JOHN G.
LAKE
ON
HEALING

Publisher's Note

This book is not intended to provide medical advice or to take the place of medical advice and treatment from your personal physician or other qualified health care professionals. Neither the publisher nor the compiler nor the compiler's ministry takes any responsibility for any possible consequences from any action taken by any person reading or following the information in this book. If readers are taking prescription medications, they should consult with their physicians and not take themselves off prescribed medicines without proper medical supervision. Each reader is solely responsible for the consequences of his or her personal choice concerning consultation with physicians or other qualified health care professionals.

JOHN G.
LAKE
ON
HEALING

COMPILED BY ROBERTS LIARDON

WHITAKER
HOUSE

Publisher's note:
The sermons, letters, and pamphlets contained here have been excerpted from
John G. Lake: The Complete Collection of His Life Teachings, which was compiled
by Roberts Liardon, originally published by Albury Publishing, and is currently
published by Whitaker House. Both Albury Publishing and Whitaker House
made all possible efforts to secure permission and to insure proper credit was
given for every entry within this book. The words, expressions, and sentence
structure of the text have been gently edited for clarity and readability.

All Scripture quotations are taken from the King James Version of the Holy
Bible. All words in *bold italics* within Scripture quotations are the emphasis of
John G. Lake.

JOHN G. LAKE ON HEALING

ISBN: 978-1-60374-162-0
Printed in the United States of America
© 2009 by Roberts Liardon

Whitaker House
1030 Hunt Valley Circle
New Kensington, PA 15068
www.whitakerhouse.com

Library of Congress Cataloging-in-Publication Data
Lake, John G.
  [Selections. 2009]
  John G. Lake on healing / by John G. Lake ; compiled by Roberts Liardon.
    p. cm.
  Summary: "A compilation of John G. Lake's sermons, letters, and other published
materials on the subject of healing, this book provides a thorough history of his healing
ministry and the life he lived for God"—Provided by publisher.
  ISBN 978-1-60374-162-0 (trade pbk. : alk. paper) 1. Healing—Religious aspects—
Christianity—Sermons.   2. Spiritual healing—Sermons.   3. Miracles—Sermons.
I. Liardon, Roberts. II. Title. III. Title: On healing.
  BT732.L25 2009
  234'.131—dc22
                                    2009026956

11 12 13 14 15 16 17 **ᴜᴊ** 28 27 26 25 24 23 22

Contents

Chapter 1

Divine Healing

∽∾⬥∾∽

I f there is something wrong with a man's spirit, he goes directly to God, but the next day he has a pain in his back, and he goes down the road to the doctor's. Where do you get your right to do such a thing?

There is a wretched looseness about consecration to God. Christians do not seem to know what consecration to God means. What would you think of Jesus Christ, if you saw Him going down the road and into a doctor's office for some dope? Why, you would feel like apologizing for the Lord, wouldn't you? Well, He has just as much reason to apologize for you. When you became a Christian with a consecrated body, soul, and spirit, your privilege of running to the doctor was cut off forevermore.

"Faith cometh by hearing, and hearing by the word of God" (Romans 10:17). This young man who testified says he suffers because of an appetite for cigarettes, and he hopes that we will pray so that the next time he wants to smoke he won't.

I tell you, God says, "Quit your sins and then come to Me, and I will pardon." He doesn't say, "You come on with your sins, and I will pardon you." He says, "You quit your meanness, you quit fooling with the doctor and the devil, you quit your secret habits and come to Me, and I will deliver you." That is the only road to God; that is the way in God.

So a Christian's consecration is not just a consecration of his spirit to God, not of his soul to God. It's a consecration of body and soul and spirit—the entire man, everything there is of us—and it cuts us forever plumb off from looking for help from the flesh, the world, or the devil.

There are three enemies of man: the world, the flesh, and the devil. Our nature has three departments: spirit and soul and body. What would you think of the Christian who would go to the devil or to some deceitful spirit to find balm for his spirit? Why, you would think he was not a Christian at all, nor would he be. Suppose a man wants peace for his soul (mind), and he appeals to the spirit of the world or the flesh to get it. You would not think he was a Christian at all. Then how will you consider a man who wants healing for his *body* and goes to the world and man to get it?

I am going to preach to you for five minutes out of the fifth [chapter] of James. He is very explicit in this matter. He is not laying down rules for the people of the world. He is talking straight to the Christians. "*Is any among you* [Christians] *afflicted? let him pray*" (James 5:13), not "let him go to the devil or the doctor or some human source."

"*Is any sick among you? Let him call for the elders of the church*" (verse 14) means this: if you have prayed and deliverance has not come, unquestionably it is a weakness of your faith. You need help. Then the next thing is, "*Let him call for*

*the elders of the church; and let them pray over him, anointing
him with oil in the name of the Lord"* (James 5:14).

When I was preaching in Washington, D.C., recently,
an old sister said she had anointed her little girl the night
before and she had put a whole bottle full of oil all over her.
So you see, she was not looking to God to heal; she expected
the anointing oil to heal. Satan is a subtle old devil, but the
Lord gives us fight. He says not the anointing of oil, but *"the
prayer of faith shall save the sick, and the Lord shall raise him
up"* (verse 15). That is why I never use oil except when requested to do so, because people are looking to the anointing
oil instead of to the Lord God. *"Let him call for the elders of
the church; and let them pray over him, anointing him with oil
in the name of the Lord: and the prayer of faith shall save the
sick,"* not the anointing oil. The use of anointing oil is a matter of obedience. It is a symbol of the Spirit of God, and that
is all it is. So we place upon the individual the anointing oil
in order that we fulfill the symbol of the Spirit of God as the
Healer, and that is all.

*"The prayer of faith shall save the sick, and the Lord shall
raise him up; and if he have committed sins, they shall be forgiv-
en him"* (verse 15). Thus, he goes on and makes the teaching
broader.

One of the beautiful things about the gospel of Jesus
Christ is that it is progressive in its revelation and application.
First, we were asked to pray if we are afflicted. Second, we
were asked to call for the elders. Then, the Lord goes down to
the real business in a man's heart. *"Confess your faults one to
another"* (James 5:16). Get your old tattling, blatting tongue
tied up, and confess to the other party that you have been
tattling.

If all the Christians had that gag in their mouths, there would not be half as much shouting in the meetings as there is. Now listen, I don't want to pound people on the head, but I want to teach you a lesson. Here is the broad principle of the gospel: *"Confess your faults."*

When I went to Africa, I had the advantage of getting on absolutely new ground that no one had spoiled with a lot of loose teaching. In this country, our people have been slobbered over with teaching that doesn't amount to anything, and they wobble this way and that way, *"like a wave of the sea driven with the wind and tossed."* And God says, *"Let not that man think that he shall receive any thing of the Lord"* (James 1:6–7).

One day, as a young man, God brought me in to see my own need when I needed healing from heaven. There was nobody to pray for me, and I was not even a Christian in the best sense of being a Christian. I was a member of a Methodist church, but I had seen God heal one dear soul, who was very dear to me. As I sat alone one day, I said, "Lord, I am finished with the doctor and with the devil. I am finished with the world and the flesh, and from today I lean on the arm of God." I committed myself to God; and God almighty, right there and then, though there was no sign of healing or anything else, accepted my consecration to Him. That disease that had stuck on my life and almost killed me for nearly nine years was gone. It was chronic constipation. I would take three ounces of castor oil at a single dose, three times a week.

The place of strength and the place of victory is the place of consecration to God. It is when a man shuts his teeth and says, "I go with God this way," that victory is going to come.

My! This wobbling business makes one think of the old Irish woman who was on a ship in a storm. When the ship rolled one way, she would say, "O good Lord," and when the ship would plunge to the other side, she would say, "Good devil." When someone asked her why she did that, she said, "Why, how can I tell into whose arms I will fall?"

May the Lord wake us up in our souls and get us out of this wobbly state and get us where we all commit ourselves once and for all and *forever* to almighty God, and then live by it and die by it.

People say, like the dear soul last night who sent word to the meeting, "I am very sick, and if I don't get deliverance, I will have to do something." Why, sure you can do something—*you can die*. You ought to die instead of insulting and denying the Lord Jesus Christ and turning your back on Him. People say, "I can't die." *Yes, you can,* if you are not a coward, *but you cannot sin.* And it is just as much a sin to commit your body to the Lord Jesus Christ and then to turn to the doctor as it is to go and commit adultery or any other sin. It is a violation of your consecration to God.

Make a consecration to God and stand by that and live by that and be willing to die by that. Then you will grow up into God, where your faith is active enough to get answers to prayer.

There is no man who lives and has the ministry of healing that could pray for all the sick people. There are so many of them. Why, you come to an assembly like this, and every old saint who has a stomachache will come and ask you to pray for them, and there is no time for anything else. God wants us to grow up into Him where we get answers to prayer for ourselves. Then, if there is an extreme case and your faith is broken, confess your faults one to another and get the rest of the people to pray for you; and then in the extreme cases, send for the elders of the church—*that* is the mind of God.

In the twelfth chapter of 1 Corinthians, the nine gifts of the Holy Spirit are enumerated.

> *For to one is given by the Spirit the word of wisdom; to another the word of knowledge by the same Spirit; to another faith by the same Spirit; to another the gifts of healing by the same Spirit; to another the working of miracles; to another prophecy; to another discerning of spirits; to another divers kinds of tongues; to another the interpretation of tongues.* (1 Corinthians 12:8–10)

These are the gifts or enablements that are given by God to certain [ones] in the church. Now, here is a thought I want to leave with you. We go over into Ephesians, and we see a different order: not the gifts of enablements are mentioned, but the gifts in this case are individuals. It is *men* to whom God has given definite ministries.

And in the church of Jesus Christ not only should the gifts exist, but also the faith to use them. And they do exist if they are developed, and they are workable when the faith in your heart is made active to use them. But you can have the gifts right out of heaven, and if the faith in your heart is not active, you cannot operate them.

There is only one prayer that is answered. It is not prayer that is answered but the prayer of faith. It is the prayer of faith that shall save the sick. Believing prayer is not much noise. Believing prayer may not be any noise at all. Believing prayer is a committing, an intelligent committing of yourself to God; and your mind is stayed in God and your heart is stayed in God and you are walking in God. You are ready to die rather than go to anyone but God. That is the real believing prayer. That is the continuous prayer. That is prevailing prayer. Blessed be God!

So in Ephesians, the Word of God tells us that there are some apostles, some prophets, some teachers, some evangelists, and some pastors. (See Ephesians 4:11.) These are God's gifts, these men—not gifts as they are mentioned in Corinthians, but men are mentioned in Ephesians—and the men with ministries are God's gift to the church until such time as they shall all come, the entire body of Christ, into the unity of the faith, into the likeness of Jesus Christ, into the measure of the stature of the Son of God. *"Till we **all** come"* (Ephesians 4:12), not one or two. Blessed be His precious name!

These things will demonstrate to you how far we are behind the gospel ideal. We are so far behind. A few years ago, many commonly believed that when the baptism of the Holy Ghost was being poured out upon the world, that we were the particular little lot who were to be the bride of Christ and go with Him when He came. But pretty soon it began to dawn on those who looked into the Word that there was not even a tangible body of Christ yet. The body of Christ is the members called of God, united in one spirit and in one hope of their calling—blessed be God—with one Lord, one faith, and one baptism. That is the body. Then all the other developments, the bride, and all the rest of it are born out of the body. (See Ephesians 4:2–6.)

God is getting a body at this present time, and in the body of Christ, the orderly body of Christ, the unified body, He wants to bring it forth today. He has set His gifts: the word of wisdom, knowledge, faith, gifts of healing, etc. He has set likewise men: apostles, prophets, evangelists, pastors, and teachers.

> *For the perfecting of the saints, for the work of the ministry, for the edifying of the body of Christ: till we all come*

> *in the unity of the faith, and of the knowledge of the Son*
> *of God, unto a perfect man, unto the measure of the stat-*
> *ute of the fullness of Christ.* (Ephesians 4:12–13)

Now healing is not a difficult matter. It does not take a bit more faith to be healed from your sickness than it does to be saved from your sins. The only difference is that in your own consciousness, you knew there was no place to get forgiveness except from God. You had sense enough to know you could not get it from the devil; you had to get it from the Lord.

But your body gets sick and your consciousness, because of your education, permits you to go to the doctor or the sorcerers or the devil, and the one is just as offensive to God as the other. The Christian body and soul and spirit are *one* [unit]. A real Christian has committed his whole being unto the living God; he has consecrated himself to Jesus Christ with all the fullness that Jesus consecrated Himself to the Father at the river Jordan. He was baptized. He consecrated Himself unto the uttermost, unto *"all righteousness"* (Matthew 3:15), unto everything that was right, unto the will of God forever. Blessed be His name.

Now there are examples in the Word of God that are very striking along this line. You listen to the Word of God: *"Cursed be the man that trusteth in man"* (Jeremiah 17:5). Talk about your running to the doctor. That is what the Lord thinks about it. *"Cursed be the man that trusteth in man, and maketh flesh his arm, and whose heart departeth from the* LORD.*"* And the Word of God in the fourteenth [chapter] of 2 Chronicles gives us a most remarkable example of Asa, the king of Israel, who trusted God when the great armies of their enemies came up against them. He went down on his knees before God, and he said,

Lord, it is nothing with thee to help, whether with many,
or with them that have no power: help us, O Lord our
God; for we rest on thee, and in thy name we go against
this multitude O Lord, thou art our God; let no man
prevail against thee. (2 Chronicles 14:11)

Their little handful of men conquered the whole mob.

But after a while, Asa got a disease in his feet, and the Word says his disease became exceeding great; and in his disease he trusted not the Lord, but the physicians; and Asa died. It is recorded against him as an offense against God that he failed to trust God for the disease in his feet, but instead trusted the physicians. (See 2 Chronicles 16:12–13.)

Somebody says, "Well, all right, I will commit myself to the Lord, and then of course, I will not have any more stomachache. I will just be kept, etc." Maybe you will if your faith in God stands strong enough, and perhaps you won't if it does not. But there is one thing that stands—that is, your consecration to God. If your faith fails, it does not make any difference; you stand consecrated to God just the same. If you do not get an answer to prayer, you are consecrated to God just the same; and if God almighty has got to let the devil thrash you half to death for a week or two months or longer, you take it until the [fault] that the Lord is after is out of your life and faith has conquered. Then you will learn obedience to God by the things you suffer. (See Hebrews 5:8.) That is the only way.

People go around cursing the devil all the time. [When] you go in the ways of the devil, you get crooked in your soul and proud in your heart, and that cuts you off from God, and you are left in the hands of the devil. The wisest thing to do with you is just like I did with one of my sons. I said, "Young man, you just take your own way until you bump your head against the wall." When he was hurt almost to death, he was glad to come back to his old dad to be helped out.

We know the Word of God so well, so in our proud hearts we say, "We have been baptized in the Holy Ghost," and all that kind of attitude. It is just as offensive to God as it can be, and God has just got to draw back His hand and let you go, like I did my son. And then you will come down with some old disease, and you will lay and fret and fume and cry until you get right with God and open your heart to God; then He will rebuke the devourer, and He will take the thing away. Bless God.

I used to be a member of a church where it was considered just as offensive to take medicine or go to the doctor as it was to go to the devil for health. The Christian who would run to a doctor was on a level with the adulterer or the thief. That is absolutely right. That is according to the Word of God. A whole consecration of your whole being—your body and soul and spirit—is what Jesus demands. It is what Jesus asks and, bless God, that is the only place that is worthwhile.

We go around talking and shouting about the almighty Christ and what He can do and what He is, etc. But the first time we get a stomachache, away we go to the doctor and get a dose, and the almighty Christ gets a slap in the face.

Beloved, you listen to me. If there are any people in all the world who ought to be taught of God, who ought to be walking with God, who ought to be consecrated to all the will of God, it is the Christian people, especially those who are baptized in the Holy Ghost. It ought to be absolutely unnecessary for any man at this day to even speak of these things in a public service. We ought to have been so committed from the first day to the Lord Jesus Christ that the committing of ourselves to any man for anything would be highly offensive to our spirits. And if we saw our brother or sister becoming weak and falling into the hands of man, our prayer and love and faith and sympathy ought to get under them as though they were falling into the habit of drinking whiskey again.

It is just as offensive for the Christian to take medicine as for the drunkard to take whiskey. Don't you see, beloved, the great wonderful advantage in the Christian's life of becoming cut clear and free from all dependence on the arm of man? You are cut forever from the world, from the flesh, from the devil. Bless God.

I had a friend in Africa who was greatly distressed because he could not learn to swim. Finally, one day he got drunk and walked off the docks into the sea at Cape Town into about five hundred feet of water, and he could swim after that, all right.

Don't you see, beloved, that you will never have faith in God in the world until you launch out into God, until you commit yourself to God and then either live or die? I belong to God; I am done with man, and I am done with leaning on his arm.

I know what these things are. In my home I had seven children. They were born without medicine. One dear brother testified the other night that the Lord had kept disease out of the home. It was not that way in mine. There wasn't a devilish thing that came down the road that my family did not get, from pneumonia, smallpox, and typhoid fever to a shooting accident, and God let us be tested right up and down the line.

It is one thing to get down on your knees and say, "I commit my body, my soul, my spirit to God," and it is another thing to stand by your baby until you hear it gasp, and it is another thing to close its eyes in death if necessary, but I am not going back on my Lord. That is the kind of training I got, and that is the clearness in faith my heart cries out for.

Maybe in another generation we will have a multitude of people who stand in God like giants, and we can have a manifestation of the sons of God and take the world for God and crown the Christ King of Kings and Lord of Lords.

Now, I do not preach to anybody else what I have not been through myself. I tell you, the Lord has let me go through the mill. One time I got inflammatory rheumatism, and for nine months I suffered. I guess I did. But I shut my teeth and I said, "You devil, you can't put me in bed; I won't go," and I dragged myself home, and I would get in bed and feel like crying out in my agony. At the end of nine months, God had wrought one thing in my heart: that if I died, the devil would not get me to take medicine again. One day I felt in my spirit I needed help. There was nobody there that could pray for me. So I got on a train and went to Chicago to John Alexander Dowie. One day there was a company of people like this, and when I came along, it was so packed full I could not even look into the door. After a while, there were some other people who couldn't get in. Finally an old man, an elder, came along and prayed for us out there; and as he did, I was healed from the crown of my head to the soles of my feet. Years after, he told me that was the only healing he ever had that he knew about.

I often wondered if the virtue came through the old brother or not, but God met my faith. Do you not see, to commit yourself to God means something? I tell you, it is probably going to mean some suffering someday, but that is the way of clearness, the way of truth. That is the way you can look every man in the face and say, "I am not leaning on the arm of flesh; I am going God's way."

We are such a weak, wobbly lot in these latter days. God is just trying to get some backbone in us. We come along and are baptized, and about a week after, we can find them doing all sorts of things. The Christians in the old days came down to be baptized, and as they did so, a Roman officer took their names and sent them up to Rome. Instantly their citizenship was canceled, their right of protection from Roman government was cut off, their goods were confiscated, and they were left as prey to the avarice of the people, but they got baptized just the same. Bless God.

I tell you, that is the kind of people that thirty million of them gave their lives to God in the first four centuries and were blotted out of the world in various ways. Thirty million of them! There was some Christian spirit, and there was some consecration to God in those days. It was poverty or death or sickness or prison or anything else, but it was God's way of consecration. I tell you, God will meet that kind of thing. If they lived, all right, and if they died, all right. They belonged to God, and the world ever since, for 1400 years, looks back with pride to that list of people who gave themselves to the Lord God. They put the stamp of character on the Christian world. Bless God.

All the heroes, bless God, did not live back there either. You come down to the history of Scotland, to the Covenanters. They wrote a covenant and said, "We will have nae King but Jesus," and you can see the old Scottish man shut his teeth and, opening a vein in his arm, sign the covenant with his own blood. And three hundred thousand of them gave their lives then to make that covenant good and died saying, "We will have nae King but Jesus."

Now you listen to me. I will guarantee to you that if there are fifty sick people in this room, and you commit yourselves to God in that spirit and with that reality, bless God, you won't need anybody to pray for you. You will just get well. Bless God. The devil cannot come around you when that kind of thing is in your soul.

One of my sons was dying with pneumonia once. I prayed for that fellow, and I prayed for him, and it was not a bit of good. But one day I was downtown, and I was praying about that boy, and the Lord said, "You go home and confess your sins to your wife."

And I said, "I will." I stopped and got one of the old elders to come down to my house. As we rode along, we talked together, and I said, "I have some things I want to fix up with my wife before you pray. There have been all kinds of prayer, but He won't hear." So I took my wife in the other room and told her the whole business, all there was; and we went into the other room and prayed for that son, and he was healed in a second.

I want to tell you that when Christians are not healed, as a rule, you get digging around and get the Holy Ghost to help you; and when they have vomited out all the stuff, they will get the healing.

You listen to me. Healing comes straight down from God. All man is, is a medium through which God can work. God is a Spirit; He needs embodiment. He chooses man as a body. The church is the body. *"Know ye not that ye are the temple of God, and that the Spirit of God dwelleth in you?"* (1 Corinthians 3:16). There is something that gets into your spirit or into your body that is obstructing the free flow of the Spirit of God. Get that thing out; it is between you and God.

I tell you, when you line people up so they will trust God for their bodies as they do for their souls, there will not be one half the backsliding there is now. I was a member of a body of one hundred thousand people, and I never heard of such a thing as any of them backsliding. They stood for God, and they died for God. The character was in them, and they did not know half as much about God as we do by the revelation of the Spirit in these days.

I am twice as anxious this afternoon about this great body of people here, to know whether or not they are going to commit themselves clear in God, than I am about the sick. There may be dozens in this room who are so very sick that they need God. But, beloved, listen. Suppose one of them was not healed and the rest were made clear in their consecration to God; you would have a bigger demonstration.

As fast as you get them healed, the Christians without Christ's consecration are down in their faith and becoming sick. After a while, a preacher gets to be a kind of doctor of saints in his little assembly. God does not want it. Get clear; get straight in your consecration to God. Put yourself body and soul and spirit forever in God's hands. Do it today, bless God. Do it today.

How ashamed a Christian ought to be that he is trusting in the arm of flesh or in a medicine bottle somewhere around the house! You go home and gather up the abominable stuff and put it in the alley box [a garbage pail] and then apologize to the alley box.

You cannot tell me anything about medicine. There never was a bigger humbug practiced on mankind than the practice of medicine. The biggest men in the medical world have declared it over and over again, but the mob does not pay any attention to it.

Professor Douglas McLaggen, who had the chair of medical jurisprudence, stood up among one thousand students, when asked to lecture on the science of medicine, and he said, "I am an honest man, and 'An honest man is the noblest work of God'; from the days of Hippocrates and Galen until now, we have been stumbling in the dark, from diagnosis to [illegible]." Sir Ashley Cooper, who was physician to Queen Victoria for twenty-five years, the greatest physician in Great Britain, said, "The science of medicine is founded upon conjecture and improved by murder." Dr. Magendie of Paris, who has the greatest system of diagnosis in the world, said, "We take up the attention of the patient with our medicine, while nature cuts in and makes a cure." But you cannot tell a third-rate American doctor that.

Yet, the Christian world turns its back on the Son of God and goes and puts itself in the hands of men. No man who ever lived, or ever will live, will ever reduce the subject of medicine to a science. No two doses of medicine will ever produce the same effect in your own person. You can take a dose of medicine today and another tomorrow, and you will have a different effect tomorrow than you had today.

That may be all right for the world. Why, the man who is not a Christian has got to have a physician of some kind, but the Christian can't. God cut the privilege off long ago. Bless God. "*Is any sick among you* [Christians]? *Let him call for the elders of the church*" (James 5:14). That is all the privilege the Word of God gives him. That is the way in to God, on the line of divine healing. Bless God.

Bless God, I tell you, I am just looking for the day when there will be a great, blessed, true company of men and women in this world who will stand in this through the living

God just as clear as crystal, who have cut clear off from the world, the flesh, and the devil. That is the characteristic of the church of Philadelphia all right.

God has let me see healings in every way that human eyes can see them. I have seen them come like the flash of lightning. I have seen the Spirit of God flash around the room, just like the lightning. God was there in lightning form, and the devils were cast out and the sick healed. I have seen God come as the tender bud when nobody knew He was there, and people were healed. I have seen people healed in the audiences when cancers would melt away and varicose veins were healed. Nobody prayed for them. They just put themselves in the hands of God. That is all.

There is no man who lives who can define the operations of faith in a man's heart. But there is one thing we are sure of: that when we cut ourselves off from every other help, we never find the Lord Jesus Christ to fail. If there is any failure, it is our failure, not God's. Bless God.

Finis, Thank God

Chapter 2

Divine Healing

ᗢᗣᗢᗣᗢ

Magazine Article
November 14, 1917

D ivine healing, what is it? It is healing by the Spirit of God, exercised through the spirit of man. Jesus, the Master Healer, not only healed Himself, but empowered His twelve disciples to perform the same ministry. Later, He empowered "[an]*other seventy also*" (Luke 10:1), making in all eighty-three men who practiced the ministry of healing during His earthly life.

After the resurrection of Jesus, just before His ascension, a great new commission was given to His disciples. He sent them to preach to all men everywhere, commanding them to *"preach the gospel to every creature"* (Mark 16:15), and declaring concerning those believers who were to become disciples through their ministry that,

> *these signs shall follow them that believe; In my name shall they* [believers] *cast out devils; they shall speak with new tongues;…they shall lay hands on the sick, and they shall recover.* (Mark 16:17–18)

A common fallacy in connection with the subject of healing is taught by the churches at large: namely, first, the days of miracles are past; and second, no one healed but the twelve apostles. These statements exist because of the lack of knowledge on the general subject of healing, as set forth in the Scriptures.

In 1 Corinthians, Paul set forth, in order, the various gifts of the Spirit prevalent in the church. First, the word of wisdom; second, the word of knowledge; third, faith; fourth, the gifts of healing; fifth, working of miracles; sixth, prophecy; seventh, discerning of spirits; eighth, diverse kinds of tongues; ninth, interpretation of tongues. (See 1 Corinthians 12:8–10.)

He commended the church in that "*ye come behind in no gift*" (1 Corinthians 1:7). All these various gifts of the Spirit were exercised among them.

James, in instructing Christians concerning their faith in God, said, "*Is any sick among you? let him call for the elders of the church; and let them pray over him.*" Regarding this prayer he said, "*The prayer of faith shall save the sick, and the Lord shall raise him up; and if he have committed sins, they shall be forgiven him*" (James 5:14–15). He further declared, "*The effectual, fervent prayer of a righteous man availeth much*" (James 5:16) in its working.

The writings of the church fathers for four hundred years after Christ emphasized the power of healing as known in the churches of that period. Certain sects of Christians from the days of Jesus until the present have practiced the ministry of healing—namely, the Armenians, the Waldenses of Germany, and the Huguenots; in later years, the followers of Dorothy Truedell of Switzerland and the Buchanites of South Africa; and in our own day, the Christian and

Missionary Alliance with headquarters in New York, the Church of God, and the followers of John Alexander Dowie, who maintain a city in the state of Illinois in which no doctor has ever practiced medicine and where no one employs a physician or takes medicine. They trust God wholly and solely for the healing of their bodies. And the national vital statistics show that their death rate is beneath the average of cities of the same population in the rest of the country.

Since the establishment of the Spokane Divine Healing Institute in January 1915, Spokane has become the healthiest city in the United States, according to the national record. And Dr. Ruthledge of Washington, D.C., in reviewing this subject said,

> Divine healing is no longer a vagary [irrational or unpredictable idea] to be smiled at. Through its practice, the Divine Healing Institute of Spokane, Reverend John G. Lake, Overseer, has made Spokane the healthiest city in the United States. In this I do not discount all the other splendid agencies of healing, but I call attention to the fact that with the establishing of the Divine Healing Institute of Spokane, the percentage of deaths in the city was lowered to that extent that Spokane became famed as the healthiest city in the United States of America.

We are frequently asked, "What is divine healing?" "Is it Christian Science?" "Is it psychological, or is it spiritual?" We reply: "Divine healing is a portion of the Spirit of God transmitted through the spirit of man." The Spirit of God was imparted by Jesus, through laying His hands upon the sick. Again and again in the Word we read, *"He laid his hands on...them, and healed them"* (Luke 4:40; see also Mark 6:5).

Indeed, the Spirit of God so radiated through and from His personality that His clothing became impregnated by it.

The woman who touched the hem of His garment *"felt in her body that she was whole of that plague"* (Mark 5:29). Jesus discerned that *"virtue is gone out of me"* (Luke 8:46). Having faith to touch His garment, she received the power of the Spirit into her person. (See Luke 8:43–48; Mark 5:25–34.) So mighty was this power of the Spirit in the apostle Paul that we read in Acts 19 that *"from his body were brought unto the sick handkerchiefs or aprons, and the diseases departed from them, and the evil spirits went out of them"* (Acts 19:12).

Students have long since discovered a new science. This new science is known as *pneumatology,* or the science of spirit. Pneumatology is a recognition of the laws of the Spirit, a discerning of the modus operandi of the Spirit's working, its effects and powers.

Indeed, scientists have undertaken to demonstrate the psychological and physiological effects of the Spirit of God in man under certain spiritual influences and conditions. In the operation of prayer, they declare that the cortex cells of the brain expand; and as they expand, they receive and retain the Spirit of God; that through the action of the will or the desire of the heart, the Spirit is transfused through the whole personality so that the cells of the brain and the cells of the body and the cells of the blood become supercharged by divine Spirit; that this absorption and retention of the Spirit of God in the person of man produces a chemical interaction. Sometimes waves of heat sweep over individuals as hands are laid upon them and the Spirit of God is transmitted to them. Persons will sometimes burst forth in violent perspiration, so great is the chemical interaction taking place within.

Most remarkable results are obtained in this ministry. Examples:

Mrs. Daniel Carter, 27 West Courtland Ave., Spokane, was afflicted with a large tumor. Thirteen physicians examined her, estimating the tumor to weigh fifteen pounds. All agreed that there was no hope of life, except through an operation to remove the mass. She was ministered to through prayer and the laying on of hands at 4:30 in the afternoon. So remarkable and powerful was the Spirit of God in her that by eleven o'clock the following day, every trace of the tumor had vanished, and she returned to the healing rooms with her corsets on, normal in size, to show us the wonder that God had accomplished in her.

Mrs. Lamphear, of Gandy Hotel, Sprague Avenue, Spokane, was a sufferer from tuberculosis and prolapses of stomach, bowels, and uterus. She was an invalid eleven years. In addition to this she suffered violently from inflammatory rheumatism. Physicians being unable to heal her, she was advised to go to Soap Lake, wash, and try the hot baths. Baths of normal temperature had no effect upon her. She was then placed in super-heated baths, the result of which was that the poisons seemed to leave the upper portion of the body and concentrate in the left leg, causing an abnormal growth on the limb. The limb became three inches longer than the other, the foot almost an inch longer than the other. A large bone spur, as large as a medium-sized orange, grew on the inside of her knee, destroying the action of the joint.

Under divine healing ministry, the leg shortened at the rate of one inch per week, the bone on the inside of the knee entirely disappeared, and her tuberculosis was healed. All her diseases fled. She was born without the outer rim of one ear and without the lower lobe. The ear began to grow and is practically a perfect ear.

We believe that this demonstrates the mightiness of the inward working of a great force and power and should illustrate the wonderful effect produced by the introduction of the Spirit of God in power into the person.

Mrs. Mary Matheny, Johnson, Washington, was under treatment for four years at the Clarkston Cancer Institute, Clarkston, Washington, and was finally discharged as incurable. Her physicians said she had forty cancers in the bladder, the uterus, stomach, breasts, throat, mouth, root of the tongue, and also in the spine. She was brought to the Spokane Divine Healing Institute and in seven weeks returned to her home healed. Her forty cancers had vanished.

During the life of the Institute, from January 1915 to the present time, an average of one hundred persons have received ministration through prayer and the laying on of hands each day—a total of almost a hundred thousand ministrations (treatments) to date.

Every portion of the city and almost every town, village, and hamlet in the state and adjoining states have those who have thus been healed by the power of God.

The financial support of the Institute is provided for by the love offerings of those who have been blessed through the ministry. No fixed charges of any kind are made for any service. A staff of ministers, who minister to the sick through prayer and laying on of hands, are continuously in attendance. Other local churches have difficulty in maintaining one pastor and possibly an assistant. This church has ten and is continuously adding to the staff, so great has become the demand for this ministry.

Chapter 3

The Science of Divine Healing

❦❦❦

Sermon • Chicago, Illinois
July 19, 1920

O ur eyes behold the triumph of Jesus Christ, the glorious and victorious Son of God, who triumphed over death and hell; who arose triumphant, salvation to obtain; that we might behold gladness and joy, and walk triumphant through Jesus Christ, through the blood that washes *"whiter than snow"* (Psalm 51:7).

"In him was life; and the life was the light of men" (John 1:4). This Scripture reveals the difference between Christianity and philosophy. Some are inquiring why it is that there is always that keynote in my addresses.

God gave me the privilege of intimacy with the philosophic East, where multitudes are ministered to by Buddhist, Confucianist, and Brahman priests. Every cult imaginable has its representatives there. I was amazed to discover that many in the Western world were gradually assimilating the philosophies of the East.

When you take the modern philosophies—Christian Science, New Thought, Unity, Divine Science, etc.—today and examine them, you discover that they are the same old philosophies of India, Egypt, and China from time immemorial. They were constructed before the Redeemer came, so there is no redemption in them. They are an endeavor to redeem one's self through self-effort.

As I said before, the difference between philosophy and religion, particularly the religion of Jesus Christ, is in the words I quoted from the Scriptures: *"In him was **life**, and the life was the light of men."* Philosophy is light; it is the best light the individual possessed who framed the philosophy, but it is not a *life giver*.

But from the soul of Jesus there breathed a holy life of God that comes into the nature of man, quickens him by its power, and by the grace of God, he has the life of Jesus in him, eternal light, eternal life. Bless God.

Many of the ancient philosophies have light. It is said by some writers that one of the Indian philosophies, the *Bhagavad Gita*, was written eight hundred years before Isaiah. It predicts the coming of Krishna, a son of God, not *the* Son of God. Listen to this philosophic jewel:

Never the spirit was born.
The spirit shall cease to be never.
Never was time it was not.
End and beginning are dreams.
Birthless and deathless and changeless
Remaineth the spirit forever;
Death hath not changed it at all,
Dead though the house of it seems.

Yet no knowledge of redemption and no knowledge of a redeemer is there.

Buddha presented his philosophy five hundred years before Jesus. The philosophies of Egypt tell the story of the flood and were written thousands of years before Jesus Christ. In the writings of each one of them, you will find many of the teachings of Jesus. The teachings of Jesus were not unique in that they were new; rather, they were new in that they contained something that none of the rest possessed. It was the divine *content* in the Word of Jesus Christ that gave His teachings their distinguishing feature from the other philosophies. That content is the *life of* God. *"In him was* **life**, *and the* **life** *was the light of men."*

The philosophies were man's best endeavor to find an explanation of life. Without knowledge of a redeemer, they were written before Christ was manifest in the world. Their authors denied the power of sin or nullified its influence as they failed to conceive of a redeeming grace, an in-working of God in man, through the Spirit of Christ, to save from sin's power and change his nature. But there is given unto us *"exceeding great and precious promises: that by these ye might be partakers of* **the divine nature**" (2 Peter 1:4).

Beloved, the real Christian, and the real Christian church, undertakes to bring to mankind the life of the Lord Jesus, knowing that when the *life* of Jesus comes, the illumination of the soul, the light of civilization, and Christianity will follow, but the *life* is first.

As men wandered from God, and as the world neglected God, men naturally fell into their own consciousness and soul states and proceeded in the common way of the world to endeavor to bless the world through light—but light never saved a world. Light never will save a world. There must be a divine content from on high that comes to the soul to enrich it and to empower it, to illuminate it and to glorify it, and more, to *deify* it. For God's purpose through Jesus Christ is to deify the nature of man and thus forever make him like unto Christ, not only in his outward appearance and habits of life, but in nature and substance and content, in spirit and soul and body, *like the Son of God.*

Jesus never intended Christians to be an imitation. They were to be bone of His bone and blood of His blood and flesh of His flesh and soul of His soul and spirit of His Spirit. And thus, He becomes to us Son of God, Savior and Redeemer forever, and we are made one with Him both in purpose and being.

Interpretation of a Message in Tongues:

Our Father God, to Thee we give the praise of our hearts, that by Thy grace we have been privileged to live in a world where not only the light of God was known, but where the life of God has come. We bless Thee that we have the privilege of living in a day when the life of God in a new flood of power and glory from heaven is coming upon a city and parched and barren world. And we thank Thee that this life of God has been in our hearts the holy water of life, blessing and enriching our nature, filling us with Thy divine grace and power through Jesus Christ the Lord.

Throughout my life, a spirit of investigation predominated. It has never been easy to accept truth readily, until my soul stepped out inch by inch and proved the ground. When approaching this matter of baptism of the Spirit it was with great care, but as a hungry soul. My heart was hungry for God. And one day the Spirit of the Lord came upon me, God flooded my life and baptized me in His Holy Spirit, and then a new and powerful working of God began in my heart which has gone on for fifteen years, until Christ has become in my world a divine reality.

Having formal acknowledgment as a student of science, it is my privilege to attend clinics, which I frequently do. I submitted myself at one time to a series of experiments. It was not sufficient to know that God healed; I had to know *how* God healed. I visited one of the great experimental institutions and submitted myself for a series of experiments.

First, they attached to my head an instrument to record the vibrations of the brain. This instrument had an indicator that would register the vibrations of the mind. So I began by repeating soothing things like the Twenty-third Psalm, calculated to soothe the mind and reduce its vibrations to the lowest point. Then I repeated the Thirty-seventh Psalm, then the thirty-fifth [chapter] of Isaiah, then the Ninety-first Psalm, then Paul's address before Agrippa. After this, I went into secular literature and recited Tennyson's "Charge of the Light Brigade" and last, Poe's "The Raven," with a prayer in my heart that at the psychological moment, God would anoint my soul in the Holy Ghost.

My difficulty was that while the reciting went on, I could not keep the Spirit from coming upon me, and when I got through with Poe's "The Raven," they said, "You are a phenomenon. You have a wider mental range than any human being we have ever seen." In reality that was not so. It was because the Spirit of God kept coming upon me in degree, so I could feel the moving of the Spirit within me.

But I prayed in my heart, *Lord God, if You will only let the Spirit of God come like the lightnings of God upon my soul for two seconds, I know something is going to happen that these men have never seen before.*

So, as I closed the last lines, suddenly the Spirit of God struck me in a burst of praise and tongues, and the old indicator on the instrument bounced to its limit, and I haven't the least idea how much further it would have gone if it were a possibility. The professors said, "We have never seen anything like it."

I replied, "Gentlemen, it is the Holy Ghost."

Now, in order to get the force of this lesson, it is necessary to give you the latest theory of the process of digestion. You will see the assimilating power of your nature, your capacity to assimilate God and take the life of God into your being and keep it in your being. I am not talking about what I believe; I am talking about what I *know*.

For many years God kept me so that sickness and death could not touch me, from the day that I saw in the ninety-first Psalm a man's privilege of entering into God, not only for healing, but also for *health* and having God and the life of God in every fiber of his being.

Scientists tell us that in a single inch of a man's skin there are one million, five hundred thousand cells, and they have almost doubled that statement now. But be that as it may, the whole structure of a man's being is one wonderful cellular structure. Your blood, your body, your brain, your bone is just one great cellular structure.

According to the latest theory on the process of digestion, the food we eat is reduced to vegetable lymph and is then absorbed into the body cells. But no scientist in the world has ever been able to satisfactorily explain what it is that changes the lymph and makes it *life*. Something happens when it is in the cells that changes it to life. This is transmutation.

I want to tell you what grew up in my soul and how I proved the fact. I could feel sometimes while in the attitude of prayer, just as you have felt hundreds of times, the impulse of the Spirit moving through my brain and my person to the tips of my fingers, just little impulses of God's presence in my life. And I said, "If there was an instrument powerful enough, I believe men could see the action of the brain cells and see what takes place."

Here is the secret of digestion: from the spirit-mind of man and through the spirit of man, there is imparted to every cell of your body impulses of spirit, waves of life. It is the movement of the Spirit. Spirit impulses pass from the cortex cells of the brain to the very ends of your fingers and toes, to every cell of the body. And when they touch that vegetable lymph in the body cells, it is transformed into *life*. That is transmutation.

In the electrical world you can dissolve zinc, and the electrical current absorbs it and transmits it to the other end of the wire. In an experiment in California, they dissolved zinc in the battery at the one end, transmitted the zinc to the other end of the wire, and deposited and solidified it at the other end of the wire, a distance of twelve miles. How is it done? There is a process of transmutation. That is what it is called. It is a change from one form to another.

My brother, listen. If that is not true in the spiritual world, there is no such thing as divine *life*; there is no such thing as salvation through the Son of God, for that which is soulish or natural must be transformed by the Spirit of God in us until it becomes spiritual—until it is of God. *"Ye must be born again"* (John 3:7) is a truly scientific statement.

Jesus sat with His disciples and ate with them, both bread and fish. He went to the Mount and ascended before them to glory, while their eyes beheld. What happened to the fish and the bread that He had eaten? I tell you there is transmutation. That which is natural becomes spiritual. That which was natural was changed by the power of God into the life of God, into the nature of God, into the substance of God, into the glory of God.

In the second experiment, they attached to my head a powerful X-ray with microscopic attachments in order to see, if possible, what the action of the brain cells were. Then I proceeded, just as in the former experiment. First, I repeated Scriptures that were soothing and calculated to reduce the action of the cortex cells to their lowest possible register. Then, I went on into the Scriptures to the better and richer things, until I came to the first of John; and as I began to recite that and the fires of God began to burn in my heart, presently, once again the Spirit of God came upon me, and the man who was at my back touched me. It was a signal to keep the poise of soul until one after another could look through the instrument. And finally when I let go, the Spirit subsided. They said, "Why, man, we cannot understand this, but the cortex cells expanded amazingly."

Oh, beloved, when you pray, something is happening in you. It is not a myth; it is the action of God. The almighty God, by the Spirit, comes into the soul, takes possession of the brain, manifests in the cortex cells, and when you will and wish (either consciously or unconsciously) the fire of God, the power of God, that *life* of God, that nature of

God, is transmitted from the cortex cells of the brain, throbs through your nerves, down through your person, into every cell of your being, into every cell of your brain and blood and flesh and bone, into the million, five hunched thousand cells in every square inch of your skin, and they are alive with God. That is divine healing.

Men have treated the gospel of Jesus Christ as though it were a sentiment and foolishness. Men who posed as being wise have scorned the phenomenon taking place in the Christian every day. But beloved, no dear old mother ever knelt before the throne of God and raised her heart to heaven without demonstrating the finest process of divine wireless transmission.

In these days, they are now able to transmit by wireless from six to seven thousand miles and even twelve thousand miles recently. Once again, they have been able to demonstrate that in one-tenth of a second they can transmit the first section of thought twelve thousand miles. Think of it! There is practically no such thing as time; it is practically done instantaneously. This explains instantaneous salvation and instantaneous healing.

Beloved, the very instant your soul moves with your heart cry and your nature yearns after God, it registers in the soul of Jesus Christ, and the answer comes back. So Jesus said, "*What things soever ye desire, when ye pray, believe that ye receive them, and ye shall have them*" (Mark 11:24), and "*While* [ye] *are yet speaking, I will hear*" (Isaiah 65:24).

I said to them, "Gentlemen, I want you to see one more thing. You go down in your hospital and bring the man who has inflammation in the shinbone. Take your instrument and attach it to his leg; leave space enough to get my hand on his leg. You can have it attached on both sides." So when the instrument was all ready, I put my hand on that man's shin, and I prayed just like Mother Etter prays, just as you all pray. No strange prayer, but the cry of my heart to God. I said, "God, kill the devilish disease by the power of God. Let the Spirit live in him; let it move in him."

Then I said, "Gentlemen, what is taking place?"

They replied, "Every cell is responding."

Beloved, all there is to healing is that the *life* of God comes back into the part that is afflicted, and right away the blood flows, the congested cells respond, and the work is done. That is again God's divine science in healing.

My soul long ago grew tired of men treating the whole subject of Christianity as though it were child's play. We have our physical sciences; we have our psychological sciences, the structure of the body and the action of the mind taught in the great schools of the land. But there is something greater. One of these days there is going to be a new chair in our universities. It will be the chair of pneumatology, the science of spirit, by which men will undertake to discover the laws of the spirit of man and the action of God through man. And by the grace of God, men shall know that God is alive and that the living Spirit of God is no dream; and its wondrous power in man and through man will be revealed.

In my healing rooms in Spokane, a dear woman came one day whose name is Lamphear. She was the wife of a merchant in the city. She had fallen down some stairs, causing a prolapse of the stomach, bowels, and uterus. She had been an invalid for eleven years. On top of this, she became tubercular unto death. On top of that, the poor woman developed inflammatory rheumatism, until she lived in a hell of torture. The physicians said there was nothing they could do for her, but advised that they take her to Soap Lake, Oregon, and perhaps the baths would do her some good.

So they put her in the hot baths there, and she suffered just as much as ever. Then they tried super-heated baths, and they put her in water hotter than any human being had ever been in before—so the superintendent testified. The result was that instead of having any healing effect, the left leg developed an abnormal growth, and it became three inches longer than the other leg, and a bone spur larger than an orange grew on the inside of the knee, destroying the action of the knee joint. The foot became an inch longer.

She came away from the institution worse than she went. She got as far as Portland. Her parents were living at The Dalles. She wanted to see her patents before she died, so her husband carried her in his arms to the boat. As he did so, a Pentecostal missionary stepped up and said, "Dear woman, we understand now *why* God told us to take this boat. He told us last night to take the eight o'clock boat for The Dalles." He called up on the telephone and found that the fare was $1.80, and as that was all the money they had, they went without their breakfast so as to be able to take the boat.

As she lay crying with her suffering (they were timid folks), the man said, "When we get to The Dalles, we will pray for you." Eventually, they reached The Dalles and went to a hotel. The two knelt to pray for her, and she says that as they prayed and put their hands on her knees, that their hands became illuminated until they looked like the hands of Jesus, their faces looked like the face of Jesus, and she was afraid. But something happened. The pain went out of her.

Strangely, she retained her tuberculosis, and the struggle for breath went on. The leg remained the same length. When she examined herself, she was surprised to discover that it was not shorter. She said, "Pray again that the Lord may make it the same length as the other," but the poor missionary was staggered.

He said, "Dear Sister, the pain is gone, you should be satisfied and give praise to God."

So she went on for three-and-a-half years, coughing her lungs out and her one leg three inches longer than the other. One day she came to the healing rooms and was ministered to. The healing action of God took place, and she felt wonderfully relieved. She said, "I can breathe clear down into my stomach."

The minister said, "What makes you limp?"

She replied, "There is a big lump on the inside of my knee, and my leg is three inches longer than it should be."

He said, "I'll pray for that."

But she said, "The missionary who prayed for me told me I should be satisfied if the pain was gone."

The minister said, "He had not grown up in God yet." And he put his hands on the lump and prayed, and God almighty dissolved that lump of bone and that leg shortened at the rate of one inch a week. The foot also shortened to its proper length, and she wears shoes like anyone else, the same on both feet. She was born without the outer rim and lobe on one ear, and it also grew and became like the other.

There is a difference between healing and miracle. Healing is the restoration of diseased tissue, but miracle is a creative action of the Spirit of God, creating that which is deficient in a man's life. And the salvation of a soul is a divine miracle of God. Every time Christ speaks the word of life to a man's heart, there is a divine, creative miracle of God wrought in him, and he is a new man in Christ Jesus.

One day I sat in Los Angeles, talking to old father Seymour. I told him an incident in the life of Elias Letwaba, one of our native preachers who lived in the country. I came to his home, and his wife said, "He is not home. A little baby is hurt, and he is praying for it." So we went over, and I got down on my knees and crawled into the native hut. I saw he was kneeling in a corner by the child. I said, "Letwaba, it is me. What is the matter with the child?" He told me that the mother had it on her back in a blanket, as natives carry their children, and it had fallen out. He said, "I think it has hurt its neck."

I examined it and saw that the baby's neck was broken, and I said to Letwaba, "Why, Letwaba, the baby's neck is broken." It would turn like the neck of a doll from side to side. I did not have faith for a broken neck, but poor old Letwaba did not know the difference. I saw he did not understand, but he discerned the spirit of doubt in my soul, and I said to myself, "I am not going to interfere with his faith. He will just feel the doubt generated by the old traditional things I ever learned. So I will go out."

And I did. I went and sat in another hut and kept on praying. I lay down at one AM; at three Letwaba came in. I said, "Well, Letwaba, how about the baby?"

He looked at me so lovingly and sweetly and said, "Why brother, the baby is all well. Jesus did heal the baby."

I said, "The baby is well! Letwaba, take me to the baby at once."

So we went to the baby, and I took the little black infant on my arm, and I came out praying, "Lord take every cursed thing out of my soul that keeps me from believing the Lord Jesus Christ." And Mr. Seymour, to whom I had related the incident, shouted, "Praise God, brother, that is not healing, it is *life!*"

In my meeting in Spokane is a dear man who came from Texas, Reverend Julias Allen. He told us he was dying of pellagra.[1] He came to Sister Etter's meeting at Dallas. On the train he apparently died, and they laid his body in the station house, covered him with gunnysacks, but discovered in the morning that he was still alive. So they carried him to Mother Etter's meeting, and she came down off the platform and prayed for him, rebuking that devil of pellagra. That man is living and has been preaching the gospel for seven years at Spokane.

Why, there is more science in the mind of God in five minutes than the bloated scholarship of the world ever knew. *"In Him is life, and the life was the light of men"* (John 1:4). The life of God is that which the mind of men and the keenest of them never knew and never understood. *"The world by wisdom knew not God"* (1 Corinthians 1:21). They could not discern the value in His death or understand the marvels of His life or why the Lord Jesus came and lived and died and entered into Hades and destroyed the power of darkness and death that held the souls of men; or how He liberated them from the chains of darkness, translated them to His own glory, and came forth to speak God's Word and reveal God's power and show God's nature. And by the grace of God, man has been privileged to enter into the nature of Jesus, and the fires of God burn in his soul like they burned in the soul of the risen Lord. That explains resurrection faith and resurrection power.

---

[1] *pellagra:* a disease marked by dermatitis, gastrointestinal disorders, and mental disturbances and associated with a diet deficient in niacin. *Merriam-Webster's 11th Collegiate Dictionary* CD-ROM, © 2003.

The scientific world has been startled by one of the English scientists, who says he has a formula for transmutation of the grosser metals into gold. The old alchemists claimed to know this secret, but somehow it disappeared from the world. Now it is claimed it can be done again—that they can take lead and silver and iron and transmute, or change, them into gold.

Beloved, that is the thing that Jesus Christ has been doing all the time. It is as old as Christianity; it is as old as the Son of God. He has been coming to the hearts of men, taking the old base conditions of the nature, injecting His life into them, inducting His power into the man, and through the mighty action of the Holy Ghost, they have been changed into the pure gold of God. That is divine transmutation.

If there never was another blessing that came to the world through Pentecost but this one of which I am now going to speak, all the price that men paid would be as nothing. Listen! There has been more real divine research by the Holy Ghost into the nature of God and the nature of man in these last fifteen years than there ever was in any similar period in Christian history, and more intelligent discovery of God's action and working in and through man than ever before. That is God's divine laboratory of spiritual knowledge.

And when anyone comes to me with the statement that there is nothing in the baptism of the Holy Ghost but a psychological manifestation, I say, "Brother, sister, come with me and see the gems of God and the beautiful gold that has come out of the dross of dirty lives, and then you will know." Saved from sin and healed from disease—that is divine demonstration.

In my Assembly at Spokane is a real little woman who was blind for nine years. She had little teaching along the line of faith of God. She sat one day with her group of six children to discover that her dirty brute of a husband had abandoned her and his children and left her to starve. A debased human being is capable of things that no beast will do, for a beast will care for its own.

You can imagine what her little heart was like. She was crushed, broken, bruised, and bleeding. She gathered her children around her and began to pray. They were sitting on their front porch. Presently, one of them got up and said, "Oh, Mama, there is a man coming up the path and He looks like Jesus! And, oh, Mama, there is blood on His hands and blood on His feet!" And the children were frightened and ran around the corner of the house. After a while, the biggest one looked around the corner and said, "Why, Mama, He is laying His hands on your eyes!" And just then her blind eyes opened. That is divine power.

And, beloved, if we could have seen the reason, we would have seen that there were some Christians, like those at the Brooks' Home, Zion City, or some other place, who were praying the power of God on a hungry world, and Jesus Christ in His search for those who would receive, rushed to her and sent her forth to praise God and teach the gospel of Jesus.

I would not have missed my life in Africa for anything. It put me up against some of the real problems. I sat upon a mountain in Africa one afternoon and counted eleven hundred native villages within the range of my eyes. I could see the color of the grass on the mountains sixty miles away. I could see the mountains one hundred and fifty miles away, so clear was its rarefied atmosphere.

Then I began to figure, and I said, "Within the range of my eyes, there live ten million native people. They have never heard the name of Jesus. In the whole land, there are at least

one hundred million people, perhaps two hundred million."
They are being born at a tremendous rate. Do you know there
are more heathen born every day than are Christianized
in fifty years? When are we going to catch up by our present method of building schools and teaching them to read?
Never! I tell you, it will never come that way. It has got to
come from heaven by the power of God, by an outpouring of
the Holy Ghost. That is divine salvation.

That is the reason my heart rejoices in the blessed promise,
"In the last days, saith God, I will pour out of my Spirit upon **all**
flesh" (Acts 2:17). And every last one of the two hundred million unsaved people is going to hear and know of the Lord Jesus
Christ. Beloved, I would rather have a place in the kingdom of
God, praying that thing into existence and praying the power
of God upon them, than anything else in the world.

Africa is said to be the first settled country in the world,
and we believe the world is six thousand years old. Africa has
been settled for five thousand years. Two hundred or four
hundred million have died every century. Split the difference
and say that three hundred million have died every [century]
for five thousand years.

It caused me to pray and meditate. I said, "Has God no
interest in these people? And if He has an interest, why is not
something done for them? What is the matter with God?
Is God unable to help, or does He not care?" My heart was
breaking under the burden of it. I said, "God, there must be an
explanation somewhere. What is it, Lord? Tell me about it."

Then my heart grew calm, and the Spirit said, "The church,
which is His body," and I knew that was God's answer.

I said, "Yes, the church should have sent missionaries and
built schools and done this and that."

But the Spirit kept on saying, "The church, which is His body. The church, which is His body." I sat and listened to that voice repeat that sentence for a half hour.

I said, "My God, my soul begins to see. The church is the ministering presence of the Son of God in the world. The church is the generating agency of the power of God in the world. The church has been negligent in one great trust. She has not prayed the power of God out of heaven."

Then I saw what has become a conviction in my soul from that day: that there never was a soul born to God in the whole earth at any time until some soul in the world got hold of the living Spirit of God and generated that Spirit in saving grace and creative virtue and ministered it until it took possession of a soul, no difference if it was a million miles away. Thus, the life of Christ is begotten in them.

When I try to induce men to forget their little squabbles and little differences and go to praying, it is because my soul feels the burden of it. Mother Etter has been like a marshal for fifty years. The sick have been healed; people have been converted and blessed. But beloved, when I heard of Brother Brook's shutting himself up night and day to pray the power of God on a world, I said, "That is where she gets her fire; that is where it comes from to my soul; that is where it comes from to other souls—through those who pray." That is divine intercession.

Notice how beautifully this armory is lighted. The world lived in darkness for five thousand years, and they had no way of lighting a place like this except by torches or candles. But there was just as much electricity five thousand years ago as there is today. Somebody found how to handle it, discovered the laws that govern it, and learned to apply it to our need.

But to this day, there is no man who can tell us what electricity is or what its substance is. We know we can control it this way and guide it that way and make it do this and that, but what it is nobody can tell us. However, down somewhere on the river there is a machine that is called a dynamo, and it draws the electricity out of the air and transmits it over the wires. And these days, they are sending it in wireless waves.

Do you know what prayer is? It is not begging God for this and that. The first thing we have to do is to get you beggars to quit begging, until a little faith moves in your soul. *Prayer* is God's divine generator. The spirit of man is God's divine dynamo. When you go to pray, your spirit gets into motion. Not ten thousand revolutions per minute, but possibly one hundred thousand. The voltage of heaven comes to your heart, and it flows from your hands, it burns into the souls of men, and God almighty's Spirit is applied through you to their need.

Over in Indiana some years ago was a farmer who used to be a friend of Brother Fockler and myself. His son had been in South America, had a dreadful case of typhoid fever and no proper nursing; the result was that he developed a great fever sore ten inches in diameter. The whole abdomen became grown up with proud flesh, one layer on top of another layer, until there were five layers. The nurse had to lift up those layers and wash it with an antiseptic to keep the maggots out of it.

When he exposed the body for me to pray for him, I was shocked. I never had seen anything like it before. As I went to pray for him, I spread my fingers out wide and put my hand right on that cursed growth of proud flesh. I prayed God in the name of Jesus Christ to blast the curse of hell and burn it up by the power of God. Then I took the train and came back to Chicago. The next day I received a telegram saying, "Lake, the most unusual thing has happened. An hour after you left, the whole print of your hand was burned into that growth a quarter of an inch deep."

You talk about the voltage of heaven and the power of God! Why, there is lightning in the soul of Jesus. The lightning of Jesus heals men by its flash; sin dissolves, disease flees when the power of God approaches.

And yet we are quibbling and wondering if Jesus Christ is big enough for our needs. Let's take the bars down. Let God come into your life. And in the name of Jesus your heart will not be satisfied with an empty Pentecost, but your soul will claim the light of God, and the lightning of Jesus will flood your life. Amen.

Chapter 4

The Truth about Divine Healing

Newspaper Articles · Sacramento, California
July–August 1927

Note: The following is a booklet that was taken from a series of articles that appeared in the newspaper Sacramento Union, *Sacramento, California, in July and August 1927. The articles were later expanded and reprinted in booklet form.*

C hapman said, just before his passing, "I believe the gift of healing is a far greater divine attainment than the gift of the evangelist." No wonder professor A. B. Bruce said in his *Miraculous Elements of the Gospel*, "Cures should be as common as conversion, and Christ's healing miracles are signs that disease does not belong to the true order of nature and are but a prophecy that the true order must be restored to us."

There is no question but what there is a universal longing for such a faith for the healing and quickening of our mortal bodies as this. Professor Bruce well expressed it in his Union

Seminary lectures, which have been a power ever since their utterance:

> What missionary would not be glad to be endowed with power to heal diseases as conferred by Jesus Christ on His disciples when He sent them on their Galilean mission? I know the feeling well. I spent part of my apprenticeship as a preacher and a missionary in a once prosperous but now decaying village in the west of Scotland, filled with an impoverished and exceptionally disease-stricken population. There I daily saw sights which awakened at once intense sympathy and involuntary loathing.
>
> There were cases of cancer; strange and demonic-like forms of insanity; children in arms, twenty years old, with the face of a full-grown man and a body not larger than an infant's. I returned home oftime sick at heart and unable to take food.
>
> What would I not have given to have had for an hour the charisma of the Galilean evangelists! And how gladly would I have gone that day not to speak the accustomed words about a Father in heaven ever ready to receive His prodigal children, but to put an end to pain, raise the dying, and to restore to soundness shattered reason. Or had I found someday, on visiting the suffering, that they had been healed, according to their report, in answer to the prayer of some saintly friend. I should have been too thankful to have been at all skeptical. I should then have seen how He Himself took our infirmities and bore our sicknesses, and we were to represent God whose supreme purpose is, as Jesus so clearly showed, to forgive all our sins and heal all our diseases.

The place of the gift of healing in the great message of Jesus' full and complete salvation has been voiced in prophetic foregleams all through the Christian centuries, as truly as the coming Messiah by the mouth of the prophets before the appearance of Jesus.

During recent years, it has broken forth in many quarters with most unusual power. As far back as 1884, Rev. R. F. Stanton, DD, a leading Presbyterian clergyman who at one time was moderator of the general assembly of the Presbyterian church, wrote in a little volume entitled *Gospel Parallelisms* these remarkable words:

> It is my aim to show that the Atonement of Christ lays the foundation equally for deliverance from sin and deliverance from disease; that complete provision has been made for both; that in the exercise of faith under the conditions prescribed, we have the same reason to believe that the body may be delivered from sickness as we have the soul may be delivered from sin; in short, that both branches of the deliverance stand on the same ground and that it is necessary to include both in any true conception of what the Gospel offers to mankind.
>
> The atoning sacrifice of Christ covers the physical as well as the spiritual needs of the race.

Colleges Lag in Science Teachings

Dr. John G. Lake defined the major branches of learning as follows:

- *Physiology* is the science of the body.
- *Psychology* is the science of the soul.
- *Pneumatology* is the science of the spirit.
- *Ontology* is the science of being.

Our schools and universities teach physiology: the laws, direction, and care of the body. In the past thirty years, psychology has found recognition so that not only the universities teach this science, but lectures on psychology are in every city and hamlet. Even business houses now give psychological courses for their employees and salesmen. Yet the psyche of man will die, and the soul is mortal. Psychology is a natural science.

What are the facts of pneumatology? Firstly, that man is triune in his nature and structure—spirit, soul, and body. Secondly, that the spirit and soul are divisible. On this question, the Bible says concerning the Word of God: *"Piercing even to the dividing asunder of soul and spirit"* (Hebrews 4:12).

Psychology—soul science—says that the soul is the seat of the affections, desires, and emotions; the active will, the self. *"My soul,"* said Jesus, *"is exceeding sorrowful"* (Matthew 26:38). *"And Mary said, My soul* [self] *doth magnify the Lord, and my spirit hath rejoiced in God my Saviour"* (Luke 1:46–47).

A type of semi-scholarship, represented by modern material scientists, has despised the Bible. No university in the United States is sufficiently advanced in scholarship to possess a chair of pneumatology.

The apostle Paul at Ephesus was received into the school of Tyrannus, a school of the Grecian philosophies. Psychology was the basis of their philosophy. Tyrannus recognized Paul's knowledge of pneumatology, the higher science, and established a chair of pneumatology. There, Paul taught the Christian philosophy, pneumatology, and psychology as Christian doctrine and experience. This resulted in the establishing of the Christian churches of Ephesus with 100,000 members. It resulted in the appointment of Timothy as the first Christian Bishop of Ephesus.

An outcome of this teaching in the school of Tyrannus was that the Grecian philosophies were discarded for the higher teaching of Christianity. From this school came Thekla, a Grecian noblewoman, a God-anointed healer, whose ministry of healing is said by students to have set a record.

And still there are those who would deny the right of Christian ministry to women.

The revelation of Jesus Christ as Savior and Healer through the simple teaching of the cross surpassed in Paul's estimation every other knowledge and led him to declare:

> *I determined not to know any thing among you, save Jesus Christ, and him crucified.*   (1 Corinthians 2:2)

> *Christ the power of God, and the wisdom of God.*
> (1 Corinthians 1:24)

> *I am not ashamed of the gospel of Christ: for it is the power of God unto salvation to every one that believeth, to the Jew first, and also to the Greek.*   (Romans 1:16)

Who has authority to pray for the sick? Is this holy ministry only given to the few? Is it a ministry to all Christians or to the clergy only? Jesus said:

> *If ye shall ask any thing in my name, I will do it.*
> (John 14:14)

> *Ask, it shall be given you; seek, and ye shall find; knock, and it shall be opened unto you.*   (Luke 11:9)

> *These signs shall follow them that believe; In my name shall they [believers] cast out devils; they shall speak*

> *with new tongues;…they shall lay hands on the sick, and*
> *they shall recover.* (Mark 16:17–18)

The apostles were commanded to go into all the world—to *make believers* in every section. The signs were to follow *the believers*, not the apostles only.

This was heaven's characteristic. It was the trademark of the Christ on *His* goods. It was the brand, the stamp burned into the soul of *the believer* with heavenly fire.

Baptism in the Spirit of Jesus was Christ reproducing Himself in *the believer:* To what extent was this reproduction to be a fact? We contend that Jesus taught that *the believer* was empowered by the Spirit's incoming and indwelling so that he was Christ's ambassador on earth. Then he must perform Christ's most holy ministries to the sinful and sick just as Jesus himself would do.

If this is true, then the believer is a priest in every respect. The believer must then perform Christ's priestly ministry.

The believer, then, is expected to heal the sick. Jesus said that a believer should lay his hands on the sick and heal them—they were not to die; they were to recover. They were healed through the believer by the power supplied from heaven by Jesus Christ to the believer.

We desire to ask, "Should the believer-priest also forgive sins or pronounce absolution to the penitent seeker after God?" We believe he should. We are sure that it is the privilege of the modern church to see this tremendous truth that was purposed by the Lord to be the glory of Christianity.

Jesus said the believer should cast out devils. He believes he should. He does it. The devil is ejected from further possession.

How did he do it? By the exercise of the bestowed power as Christ's believer-priest, he exercises spiritual authority over the devil in the candidate and frees him from control.

In this, he has performed the Christ-function. The sick likewise are healed through the believer-priest. In this also he performs another Christ-ministry. Then how about sin? Why does not the believer-priest by the same spiritual power and authority destroy the consciousness of sin in the soul and pronounce absolution for sins that are past?

We are asking these questions in order to discover what the believer's ministry as Christ's representative is.

We are not alone in our faith that the believer should perform the full ministry of the Christ:

+ "I am a priest."—Robert Browning
+ "The early church lost its power when it lost sight of its high priestly office."—Bishop Burnett
+ "The church needs to realize in new ways the inherent priesthood of Christian believers."—Lambeth Conference of Anglican Bishops, 1906
+ "The authority to pronounce absolution and remission of sins that are past and fulfill the aspirations of the soul for the future, I believe to be spiritual and not ecclesiastical and traditional, and to belong equally to everyone who has received such absolution and remission, and such gifts of the spiritual life." —Lyman Abbott (1835–1922)
+ "The experience of the Free Church confirms what we should expect from study of the New Testament and modern psychology, that the priesthood of all believers rests on sounder evidence than the priesthood of some believers."—Rev. Dr. Glover of Cambridge

+ "With the Quaker it is not that there is no clergy, but that there is no laity, for we are all priests unto the Highest."—John H. Graham in *The Faith of the Quaker*

+ "I am ever in the presence not only of a Great Power, or a Great Lawgiver, but a Great Healer."—Lyman Abbott

Therefore, every believer on Jesus Christ is authorized by the Lord to do as He has done, assured of Christ's assistance:

> *Greater works than these shall* [ye] *do, because I* [Jesus] *go unto my Father.*　　　　　　　　(John 14:12)

> *And they went forth, and preached every where, the Lord working with them, and confirming the word with signs following.*　　　　　(Mark 16:20)

> *Lo, I am with you alway, even unto the end of the world.*　　　　　　　　(Matthew 28:20)

The miracles of Jesus have been the battleground of the centuries. Men have devoted their lives in an endeavor to break down faith in miracles. Yet more believe in miracles today than ever before.

Pseudoscience declares miracles impossible. Yet the biggest men in the scientific world are believers in the supernatural and know that miracles are the discovery and utilization of which the material scientist knows nothing.

The miracle realm is man's natural realm. He is by creation the companion of the miracle-working God. Sin dethroned man from the miracle-working realm, but through grace he is coming into his own.

It has been hard for us to grasp the principles of this life of faith. In the beginning, man's spirit was the dominant force in the world; when he sinned, his *mind* became dominant. Sin dethroned the spirit and crowned the intellect. But grace is restoring the spirit to its place of dominion, and when man comes to realize this, he will live in the realm of the supernatural without effort. No longer will faith be a struggle but a normal living in the realm of God. The spiritual realm places men where communion with God is a normal experience.

Miracles are then his native breath. No one knows to what extent the mind and the spirit can be developed. This is not the power of mind over matter, but the power of the spirit over both mind and matter. If the body is kept in fine fettle, there is almost no limitation to man's development.

We have been slow to come to a realization that man is a spirit and that his spirit nature is his basic nature. We have sought to educate him along intellectual lines, utterly ignoring the spiritual, so man has become a self-centered, self-seeking being.

Man has lost his sense of relationship and responsibility toward God and man. That makes him lawless. We cannot ignore the spiritual side of man without magnifying the intellectual and physical; to do this without the restraint of the spirit is to unleash sin and give it dominance over the whole man.

There must be a culture and development of the spiritual nature to a point where it can enjoy fellowship with the Father God. It is above mind as God is above nature.

Man's intellect is ever conscious of supernatural forces that he cannot understand. He senses the spirit realm and longs for its freedom and creative power, but cannot enter until changed from self and sin; the spirit must be enthroned and in action rather than the intellect—spirit above *both* mind and matter.

God Destroys Sin—Sin Is Death

Does God always heal? *"In him is no darkness at all"* (1 John 1:5). Can darkness come out of light? Can sickness come out of health? Is death born of life?

The issue resolves itself into this: Of what is the redemption of Jesus Christ constituted? What existing powers does He promise to destroy?

First, sin. When Christ's redemption is completed, sin is gone. *"By one man sin entered into the world, and death by sin"* (Romans 5:12). Death entered into the world through sin.

Sickness is incipient death, death in process.

Jesus *"went about doing good, and healing all that were oppressed of the devil"* (Acts 10:38). In Luke chapter thirteen, Jesus demanded His right to heal the woman bowed together with the spirit of infirmity as follows: *"And ought not this woman, being a daughter of Abraham, whom Satan hath bound, lo, these eighteen years, be loosed from this bond* [be healed] *on the sabbath day?"* (Luke 13:16); and overriding traditions of the Jews, He healed her then and there.

> *The last enemy that shall be destroyed is death.*
> (1 Corinthians 15:26)

> *For this purpose the Son of God was manifested, that he might destroy the works of the devil.* (1 John 3:8)

Sin, sickness, and death are doomed, doomed to death by the decree of Christ Jesus. Sin, sickness, and death are the devil's triumvirate—the triple curse.

Heaven is the absence of this triple curse; heaven is sinlessness, sicklessness, and deathlessness. This is the ultimate of Christ's redemption.

Dr. Frank N. Riale, field secretary for the Presbyterian department of education, is the author of one of the greatest books of the century, *The Antidote for Sin, Sickness, and Death*:

> Today, science labors to eliminate sickness and declares, "There is no reason why men should die." Science declares men are so constructed as to be perpetually renewed. Many great scientists declare the elimination of sickness to be their final objective.
>
> Jesus anticipated the world's need. He commanded His power for the use of mankind and invites us to help ourselves to His eternal quality and become, thereby, sons of God.

The Love of Jesus Healed the Sick, Afflicted

Take the shackles off God.

Jesus did not heal the sick in order to coax them to be Christians. He healed because it was His nature to heal. The multitude surrounded Him. His love gushed forth like an electric billow. *"There went virtue out of him, and healed them all"* (Luke 6:19).

Some modern evangelists have degraded divine healing by making it a teaser to bring those desirous of healing under the sway of their ministry. Jesus healed both saint and sinner—to the dismay of His apostles, who had not yet grown to the soul stature of Jesus. They reported to Jesus:

> *"We saw one casting out devils in thy name, and he followeth not us: and we forbad him, because he followeth*

> *not us." But Jesus said, "Forbid him not, for there is no*
> *man which shall do a miracle in my name, that can light-*
> *ly speak evil of me."* (Mark 9:38–39)

He met a man at the pool of Bethesda, a paralytic. This man did not ask for healing. Jesus went to him and said: *"Wilt thou be made whole?"* (John 5:6). Here Jesus was asking for the privilege of healing the sufferer. He healed him. His love compelled it.

Later, Jesus met the healed man in the temple and said: *"Behold, thou art made whole: sin no more, lest a worse thing come unto thee"* (John 5:14).

Jesus' action is a perpetual rebuke to the priestcraft who endeavor to use the possibility of the individual's healing as a means to force him into the church.

The outgushing of His love for the world burst all bounds, and four times He healed multitudes. But some say: "This was Jesus. No apostle had such an experience."

When Peter went down the street as the evening shadows fell, when his shadow reached across the street, *"they brought forth the sick into the streets, and laid them on beds and couches, that at the least the shadow of Peter passing by might overshadow some of them"* (Acts 5:15). The clear inference is that they were healed.

James, writing to the twelve tribes scattered abroad—not the little group of Jews constituting the kingdom of the Jews, but the whole body of the nation of Israel scattered throughout the world, both the ten-tribed kingdom and the two-tribed kingdom—shouts: *"Is any sick among you? let him call for the elders of the church; and let them pray over him"*—not prepare him for death—but that *"if he have committed sins,*

they shall be forgiven him" (James 5:14–15). He is coming into
His own.

Healing was the evidence of God's forgiveness, heaven's
testimony that their sins were remembered no more.

Take the shackles off God. Enlarge your theologies to
Christ's standard, and the world will love and worship Him
forever.

Jesus' Healings Were Not Always Instant

Faith Is a Large Factor in Regaining Health

In one of the letters received from readers, this question
is asked: "Why are not all persons healed instantly, as Jesus
healed?"

The writer of this letter is mistaken in thinking that Jesus
always healed instantly. A case in point is the healing of the
ten lepers; as they went, they were cleansed. (See Luke 17:14.)
The healing virtue was administered. The healing process became evident later.

Again, Jesus laid His hands on a blind man and then inquired, "What do you see?" The man replied, "I see men as
walking trees." His sight was still imperfect. Then Jesus laid
His hands on him the second time and he saw clearly. (See
Mark 8:23–25.)

Healing is by degree, based on two conditions: first,
the degree of healing virtue administered; second, the degree of faith that gives action and power to the virtue
administered.

> *The word preached did not profit them, not being mixed
> with faith in them that heard it.* (Hebrews 4:2)

God Passes on Powers to Cure to All Followers

Jesus not only healed the sick, but performed a creative miracle on the man born blind. (See John 9.) Being born blind, it is self-evident the eyes were not a finished creation. Otherwise, he would have seen. The narrative reveals that the blind man did not know who Jesus was. Jesus did not make Himself known until after the miracle had been performed. Let us analyze the incident.

Jesus discovered the man born blind. (See verse 1.) He then spat on the ground and made clay of the spittle. Why? Because Jesus was a fundamentalist. The story of creation in Genesis says that *"God formed man of the dust of the ground"* (Genesis 2:7). Jesus, in finishing the creation of the eyes, adopted the same method. He stooped down, took up some dust, spat on it, and put it on the blind man. This was not healing. It was a work of creation.

In 1 Corinthians, the twelfth chapter, it is said that in distributing the gifts of the Spirit to the members of the church, one was given the *"gifts of healing…*[and] *to another the working of miracles"* (1 Corinthians 12:9–10). Healing is the renewal of the body from diseased conditions. A miracle is in the creative order. The case of the blind man was an exercise of creative authority, not the restoration of diseased tissue. The man was made whole.

The grouchers made their kick. The Pharisees examined the man and asked, "Who healed you?"

He answered, *"I know not"* (John 9:12).[2]

It is clearly evident to students of divine healing that sometimes the Spirit of God is ministered to the sick person to a

---

[2] Note: The biblical account says that the blind man answered that Jesus had healed him, but when asked where Jesus was, he answered, *"I know not."*

degree that he is manifestly supercharged with the Spirit. Just as a person holds a galvanic battery until the system is charged with electric force, yet no real and final healing takes place until something occurs that releases the faith of the individual, a flash of divine power is observed, a veritable explosion has taken place in the sick person, and the disease is destroyed.

This tangibility of the Spirit of God is the scientific secret of healing.

A diseased woman followed Jesus in a crowd. She knew the law of the Spirit and had observed that it flowed from the person of Jesus and healed the sick. She was convinced it must also be present in His clothing. So she reasoned: "If I could but touch the hem of His garment, I would be made whole." (See Mark 5:28; Matthew 9:20–21.) She did so. She was healed of a twelve-year sickness that had baffled physicians and left her in poverty.

Jesus was aware that someone had been healed. He turned to ask who it was. Peter said, "See how the multitude is thronging and jostling You."

But Jesus answered, "Someone has touched Me, for I perceive that virtue has gone out of Me." Jesus was aware of the outflow.

The woman was aware of the reception. Her healing was a fact. (See Mark 5:25–34.) Here, faith and the power of God were apparent. It was a veritable chemical reaction. Healing always is.

I believe the reason that people do not see the possibilities of divine healing is that they are not aware of its scientific aspects. The grace and love of God in the soul opens the nature to God. The Spirit of God resounds.

When the Pharisees asked the man who had been born blind, "What do you think of Him?" he replied, *"He is a prophet"* (John 9:17).

Later, Jesus found him and said to him, *"Dost thou believe on the Son of God?"* (verse 35).

The man replied, *"Who is he, Lord, that I might believe on him?"* (verse 36).

Jesus answered, *"I that speak unto thee am he."* (See John 37.)

The struggle of the centuries has been to free the soul of man from narrow interpretations. Jesus has sometimes been made to appear as a little bigot, sometimes as an impostor. The world is still waiting to see Him as He is: Jesus the magnificent, Jesus the giant, Jesus the compassionate, Jesus the dynamic—the wonder of the centuries.

Take the shackles off God. Let Him have a chance to bless mankind without ecclesiastical limitations.

As a missionary, I have witnessed the healing of thousands of heathens. Thus was Christ's love and compassion for a lost world revealed. And thus, the writer was assisted into the larger vision of a world-redeemer whose hand and heart are extended to God's big world, and every man—saint and sinner—is invited to behold and love Him.

Jesus Used Science to Heal the Afflicted

The Law of Contact and Transmission Was the Medium through Which the Master Wrought Miracles

Mrs. John W. Goudy of Chicago writes, "How can you speak of divine healing as scientific if healing is through the atonement of Jesus Christ? How can the matter of atonement and grace be considered scientific?"

Atonement through the grace of God is scientific in its application. Jesus used many methods of healing the sick. All were scientific. Science is the discovery of how God does things.

Jesus laid His hands upon the sick in obedience to the law of contact and transmission. Contact of His hands with the sick one permitted the Spirit of God in Him to flow into the sick man.

The sick woman who touched His clothes found that the Spirit emanated from His person. She touched the *"hem of His garment"* and the Spirit flashed into her. She was made whole. (See Mark 5:27–29.) This was a scientific process.

Paul, knowing this law, laid his hands upon handkerchiefs and aprons. The Bible says that when they were laid upon the sick, they were healed, and the demons went out of those possessed. Materialists have said this was superstition. It is entirely scientific. The Spirit of God emanating from Paul transformed the handkerchiefs into "storage batteries" of Holy Spirit power. When they were laid upon the sick, they surcharged the body, and healing was the result. (See Acts 19:12.)

This demonstrates, firstly, that the Spirit of God is a tangible substance, a heavenly materiality. Secondly, it is capable of being stored in the substance of a handkerchief, as demonstrated in the garments of Jesus or in the handkerchiefs of Paul. Thirdly, it will transmit power from handkerchiefs to the sick person. Fourthly, its action in the sick man was so powerful that the disease departed. Fifthly, the demonized also were relieved. Both the sick and insane were healed by this method.

While the scientific mind always asks "how" and "why," it is not necessary for the soul desiring Christ's blessing to have any knowledge of the scientific process by which healing or salvation is accomplished.

Jesus said, *"He that receiveth me"* (Matthew 10:40; John 13:20). Men receive Jesus Christ into the heart as one receives a lover. It is an affectionate relationship. Men obey Him because they love Him. They obey Him because they have received Him affectionately. He has become their souls' lover.

His love and power in them redeems them from sin and sickness and eventually, we are promised in His Word, He will also redeem us from death. Redemption from sin, sickness, and death constitutes man's deliverance from bondage to Satan and his kingdom (see Hosea 13:14), and establishes the kingdom of heaven.

The Bible Shows Jesus Healed the Sick by His Word

Exercised Authority over Disease by Speaking to Those Afflicted

Yesterday we discussed Jesus healing through the laying on of hands. Today we will examine Jesus healing by the word command, and other methods.

> *They brought to him a man sick of the palsy, lying on a bed: and Jesus seeing their faith* [the faith of those who brought the man as well as that of the man himself] *said unto the sick of the palsy; Son, be of good cheer; thy sins be forgiven thee.* (Matthew 9:2)

The scribes thought to themselves, "*This man* [Jesus] *blasphemeth*" (verse 3). Jesus met this opposition by saying,

> *Wherefore think ye evil in your hearts? For whether is easier, to say, Thy sins be forgiven thee; or to say, Arise, and walk? But that ye may know that the Son of man hath power on earth to forgive sins, (then saith he to the sick of the palsy,) Arise, take up thy bed, and go unto thine house.* (Matthew 9:4–6)

The man arose and walked. No hands were laid on this man. There was no external ministry of any kind. Jesus commanded; the man was healed.

They brought a man who was dumb [mute], possessed of a devil. When the devil was cast out, the man spoke. The people wondered. This also is His exercise of spiritual authority. (See Matthew 9:32–33.) When Jesus commanded, the power of God entered and ejected the demon.

At Capernaum a centurion came saying, "*Lord, my servant lieth at home sick of the palsy, grievously tormented.*" Jesus said, "*I will come and heal him.*" The centurion answered, "Not so. '*Speak the word only, and my servant shall be healed.*' That is enough." And Jesus said, "Go home. It is done." The record shows the servant was healed. (See Matthew 8:6–8, 13.)

Many have laughed at the idea of man being healed long distances from the one who ministers in Jesus' name. But here is a clear case, and the God-anointed may still command God's power. To the needy, distance is no barrier.

I now present mass healing. Four times it is recorded in the Gospels that "He healed multitudes; there went out a virtue from Him, and He healed them all." There was no personal touch. (See Matthew 12:15, 14:14, 15:30, 19:2.)

God is not confined to methods. Heaven bows to the soul with faith anywhere, under any conditions. *"Whosoever will, let him take of the water of life freely"* (Revelation 22:17).

Again, Jesus said, *"If two of you shall agree on earth as touching any thing that they shall ask, it shall be done for them"* (Matthew 18:19).

"Hitherto have ye asked nothing in my name: ask, and ye shall receive, that your joy may be full" (John 16:24), said Jesus.

The apostle James gave command that elders of the church should pray for the sick and anoint them with oil. Oil is the symbol of the healing Spirit. This is a command: "Pray for the sick that they may be healed." (See James 5:14–15.)

Where? Anywhere.

When? Forever. As long as Jesus Christ reigns in heaven. As long as men on earth have faith in Him.

The voice of Jesus still is heard saying, *"Whatsoever ye shall ask in my name, that will I do"* (John 14:13).

"Ask, seek, knock—find Jesus." (See Matthew 7:7–8; Luke 11:9–10.)

"With God all things are possible" (Mark 10:27), and *"all things are possible to him that believeth"* (Mark 9:23).

Divine healing through prayer is as old as the race of man. The first book of the Bible, Genesis, records the healing of the wives of a heathen king in response to the prayer of Abraham. (See Genesis 20:17.)

The second book of the Bible, Exodus, gives us the terms of a distinctive covenant between the nation of Israel and *Jehovah Rophi*, "The Lord thy Healer." In this covenant God not only agreed to heal the people when sick, but not to permit the sicknesses of Egypt to touch them. Its terms are:

> *If thou wilt diligently hearken to the voice of the* LORD *thy God, and wilt do that which is right in his sight, and wilt give ear to his commandments, and keep all his statutes* [on this condition, Jehovah agrees], *I will put none of these diseases upon thee, which I have brought upon the Egyptians: for I am the* LORD *that healeth thee.* (Exodus 15:26)

Under this covenant, the twelve-tribed nation lived without doctors or medicine for 450 years, until the nation of Israel had an army of 1,100,000, and Judah an army of 500,000. Figuring on the same basis as the number of Americans in the army during the world war, this would give Israel and Judah a combined population of between 25,000,000 and 30,000,000.

King David of Israel gave the most extraordinary health report that history records: he said, "*There was not one feeble person among their tribes*" (Psalm 105:37).

Such historic data should go far to convince the world of our day that an absolute trust in God is not only a safe policy, but a most scientific guarantee of national health.

In this connection we must examine Israel's national constitution as it was made the basis of national health. Firstly, its basic principles were the Ten Commandments. Secondly, it contained a law in which Jehovah held perpetual title to the land. Thirdly, a credit and mortgage statute. Fourthly, a distribution of surplus wealth statute. Fifthly, the most extraordinary labor law ever written. Sixthly, an absolutely equitable tax law by which every citizen paid one-tenth of his increase. (See Deuteronomy 5–26.)

This is the only national constitution given directly by Jehovah and is the foundation of all national constitutions.

For keeping this constitution, Jehovah guaranteed the nation against wars, pestilences, poverty, destructive droughts, and lastly, "I will take sickness away from the midst of thee." (See Deuteronomy 7:15.)

The broad scope of divine healing in Israel is the basis of all faith in God for healing and was the foundation of the ministry of Jesus Christ, Israel's Redeemer and the world's Savior.

Israel had been kept free of disease for 450 years through divine healing. Outside of Israel there was no divine healing. No other religion in the world possessed healing power. There is not a single instance of this power in the life of India, Egypt, China, or Africa.

The Hebrews alone, from Abraham onward, exhibited the power of healing at this time. Later, knowledge of Israel's God and His power to heal disease spread through the nations of the world.

The prophets of Israel were marvelous men of God. At their word, empires rose and fell. Life and death obeyed their will. Earth and sky answered their call. Before their eyes, future history marched with events of the present. No men of any other nation equaled them. No bibliotheca of any other nation compared with their Holy Scriptures.

Christ, God's Gift

Christ came as God's gift to Israel and Israel only. To Judah, the remnant of Israel, He came. Despite all that has been imagined and written of miracles in His childhood, there is not a particle of evidence that He performed any miracles until, at Cana of Galilee, He turned water into wine. The Bible states this miracle was the beginning of miracles by Jesus. (See John 2:1–11.)

Jesus performed no public ministry until He was thirty. The law of Moses forbade it. So we read that when Jesus was about thirty, He came to John the Baptist and was baptized. (See 1 Chronicles 23:3 and Luke 3:21–23.)

His baptism was His dedication of Himself to the heavenly Father. He dedicated body, soul, and spirit. To John He said, "Into all righteousness." (See Matthew 3:15.)

He was dedicating Himself to God to reveal the righteousness of God. Jesus' dedication was wholly unselfish. But His dedication in itself was not sufficient to qualify Him to reveal God. His humanity must be submerged in the Holy Spirit. As He was baptized in Jordan, this took place.

Now He must be tested. He was led of the Holy Spirit into the wilderness to be tempted by Satan. This was to find if His dedication was a fact or if He would fail under the forty-day test.

Three temptations were applied. Firstly, a psychological temptation to His mind—love of acclaim. Secondly, a spiritual temptation applied to His spirit—that He might by a simple acknowledgment of Satan secure *all the kingdoms of the world* (Matthew 4:8).

When He conquered, the natural result took place in Himself. Having overcome, the consciousness of inherent power was radiant in Him. *And Jesus returned in the power of the Spirit* (Luke 4:14). (See Matthew 4:1–11 and Luke 4:1–13.)

Jesus now makes the next advance; He proclaims His platform. Returning to Nazareth, He boldly declares, "The Spirit of the Lord is upon me. (1) He has anointed me to preach the gospel to the poor; (2) He has sent me to heal the brokenhearted; (3) to proclaim liberty to the captive; (4) recovering of sight to the blind; (5) to set at liberty them that are bruised; (6) to preach the acceptable year of the Lord." (See Luke 4:18–19.)

No more waiting for the release of the year of Jubilee. Jesus Christ, the Eternal Jubilee, was at hand to save and heal.

Jesus' ministry of healing and the marvelous faith in God that He exhibited in miracle working were no accident. Miracles must be His very breath, for 800 years before His birth the prophet Isaiah had proclaimed:

> *He will come and save you. Then the eyes of the blind shall be opened, and the ears of the deaf shall be unstopped. Then shall the lame man leap as an hart, and the tongue of the dumb sing.* (Isaiah 35:4–6)

So to be Savior of the world, He must be forever the miracle-worker of the ages; the death destroyer; the finality of revelation of the majesty, power, and mercy of Jesus!

+ The very name was a miracle.
+ The angel announced it.
+ Jesus' birth was a miracle.
+ His wisdom was a miracle.
+ His life was a miracle.
+ His teachings were miraculous.
+ He lived and walked in the realm of the miraculous. He made miracles common.

+ His death was a miracle.
+ His resurrection was a miracle.
+ His appearances after death were miraculous.
+ His ascension was a staggering miracle.

His pouring out of the Spirit on the day of Pentecost was the outstanding miracle. It was the one event in which His whole Saviorhood climaxed. Out of heaven was given to His followers the Spirit of the Eternal, to do in them all it had done in Him. Sin, sickness, and death were doomed.

He came as a roaring tempest, as tongues of fire crowning the one hundred and twenty as the living eternal Spirit entering into them. He proclaimed His triumphant entry into man through speaking in languages they knew not.

His deity had lifted them into His realm, transfigured, transformed, transmuted.

Jesus bestowed the power to heal upon His disciples:

Then he called his twelve disciples together, and gave them power and authority over all devils, and to cure diseases. And he sent them to preach the kingdom of God, and to heal the sick....And they departed, and went through the towns, preaching the gospel, and healing every where. (Luke 9:1–2, 6)

He likewise bestowed power to heal upon the seventy:

After these things the Lord appointed other seventy also, and sent them two and two before his face into every city and place, whither he himself would come....Heal the sick that are therein, and say unto them, The kingdom of God is come nigh unto you. (Luke 10:1, 9)

In order to be fully informed on the question of divine healing, let us study this question as part of the fully-rounded development and life of Jesus.

In beginning His revelation of the life of God for, and in, man, Jesus chose the order of nature as the realm of His first demonstration. (1) Jesus turned the water into wine. (See John 2:1–10.) (2) He stifled the waves. (See Luke 8:24.) (3) He walked on water. (See Matthew 14:25.) These revelations of power over nature each surpassed the other.

Then Jesus astounded His followers by turning to the creative life of God. He fed the multitude by an act of creative power when He created fish and bread to feed five thousand. (See Matthew 14:15–21.)

This shows the distinction between healings and miracles. Miracles are creative. Healing is a restoration of what has been.

Jesus now advances into a new sphere, the order of sickness. Here He meets the mind of the other that must be conformed to His. (1) Jesus heals Peter's wife's mother. This is first degree healing. (See Matthew 8:14–15.) (2) Jesus meets the blind man and heals him. This is second degree healing. (See Mark 8:22–26.) (3) The lepers are healed—healing in the third degree. (See Luke 17:11–19.)

Again, Jesus enters the creative realm and creates eyes in a man born blind. Blindness from birth is evidence of an unfinished condition of the eyes. The creative process was not complete. Jesus stooped, took dust from the road, spat upon it, and put it on the man's eyes. In so doing He finished a work of creation; the man saw. (See John 9:1–7.)

Now, Jesus again advances. This time He chooses the order of death. (1) He raised the daughter of Jarius, dead a few minutes. This is the first degree. (See Mark 5:22–24, 38–42.) (2) Jesus meets a funeral procession coming out of the city of Nain. He commands the young man to live, and he sat up. This man was dead many hours. This is the second degree. (See Luke 7:11–15.) (3) His friend Lazarus is dead four days. His body is in a state of decomposition. Jesus commands Lazarus to come forth. He who was dead arose. This was the third degree. (See John 11:1–15.)

Now, Jesus again steps into the creative realm and announces His coming death. He declares of His life, "I have power to lay it down, and I have power to take it again" (John 10:18).

Through this chain of successive abandonment to God, we discover the soul-steps of Jesus. Every step was taken with reliance on the Word of God as the all-sufficient guide.

Jesus took the promises of God in the Scriptures and permitted them to work out in His soul. Therefore, His promises to us are not made on His own speculation, but because of His soul's discovery of the mind of God. But He did not let it rest there. He took each discovered promise and worked it out.

He discovered the promise of supply and fed the multitude. He discovered healing power and made the blind to see, the deaf to heal, the lame to walk. He discovered the promise of "man the master" when anointed of God, and He stilled the waves and turned the water into wine; of life ever-present, and He raised Lazarus and the widow's son; of life everlasting, and He rose Himself from the grave.

He gave His promises as discovered and demonstrated truth, and He tells us these things shall be ours as we are lifted by the Spirit into the God realm, the Christ-conscious realm.

But it is the one real thing among the myriads of life's illusions and contains in itself man's future hope and his transcendent glory. Herein is the true dominion of man.

The Marvelous Experience of Christ's "Death Ministry" Produced in His Soul the Power and Glory of the Resurrection

We have followed Jesus through the continued ascents of His earthly career. Jesus has developed in faith and knowledge and "*in favour with God and man*" (Luke 2:52) at every step. If we were to stop at this point and refuse to follow Him to the throne of the universe, we would miss the whole purpose of His life. Divine healing and every other outflow of His holy soul would be beggared and perverted if we failed here.

Christianity is not a mere philosophy. It is more. It is very much more. Christianity is not simply obedience to beautiful commandments. Christianity is not only the acceptance of glorious promises. Christianity is a divine content. Christianity is a heavenly dynamic. Christianity is the ultimate of all consciousness of God. Christianity is wholly supernatural. Christianity comes down from heaven from the innermost heart of the glorified Christ. Christianity is in the innermost and uttermost of man declaring, "*I am he that liveth, and was dead; and, behold, I am alive for evermore, Amen; and have the keys of hell and of death*" (Revelation 1:18). Christianity is the spotless descent of God into man and the sinless ascent of man into God. The Holy Spirit is the agent by whom it is accomplished.

The significance of Jesus' death was not in His sacrifice only, but also in His achievement in the regions of death He took death captive. He liberated those who, in death, awaited

His coming and deliverance. Jesus took them in triumph from the control of the angel of death and transferred them to His own glory.

David prophesied, "He ascended upon high. He led captivity captive. He gave gifts unto men, even unto the rebellious also, that they might know the mercy of the Lord." (See Psalm 68:18.)

Peter declared, "Christ went and preached unto the spirits in prison, while once the long-suffering of God waited in the days of Noah while the ark was being prepared." (See 1 Peter 3:18–20.)

And lest we fail to comprehend the source of His ministry in death, Peter says again, "*For this cause was the gospel preached also to them that are dead, that they might be judged according to men in the flesh, but live according to God in the spirit*" (1 Peter 4:6).

The apocryphal book of Nicodemus relates this: "Jesus came to the regions of death, released the captives, and proclaimed liberty." (See *The Gospel of Nicodemus*[3] 6:1.)

It was this marvelous experience of Jesus in death ministry that produced in His soul the glory-power of the resurrection, not only His personal triumph over death, but the release of those held in death's chains.

In all the universe there was none with such triumph in his spirit as Jesus possessed when death's bars were broken.

---

[3] *The Gospel of Nicodemus* is considered a part of the pseudepigrapha, any of various pseudonymous or anonymous Jewish religious writings of the period 200 BC to AD 200, but are books of ancient Jewish literature outside any canon of biblical Scripture. *Merriam-Webster's 11th Collegiate Dictionary* CD-ROM, © 2003. Many, as with *The Gospel of Nicodemus*, are purported to have come from biblical characters. The pseudepigrapha provide colorful stories and some historical background and are useful in showing various concepts and beliefs held by ancient peoples in the Middle East.

With power heretofore unknown, He commanded His followers, saying, *"All power is given unto me in heaven and in earth"* (Matthew 28:18).

Glorifying in this amazing ascent in consciousness, He instantly found the eleven and breathed on them, saying: *"Receive ye the Holy Ghost"* (John 20:22). This was Jesus' endeavor to lift them into the same soul triumph that He enjoyed.

The ascension was a further advance in triumphant consciousness, climaxed by His presentation of Himself at the throne of God, where, Peter says, "He received from the Father the gift of the Holy Spirit." (See Acts 2:33.) This was Jesus' divine equipment as world Savior. From then on, He was empowered to administer the transcendent glory-power to all who would receive—divine healing, saving power. The empowering of the Christian soul from on high is the pouring forth of the Holy Spirit by Jesus Christ, High Priest of heaven.

That we may realize the uttermost of ultimate transcendence of the soul of Jesus in glory, hear Him declare anew:

> I am he that liveth and was dead; and, behold, I am alive for evermore, Amen; and have the keys of hell and of death.   (Revelation 1:18)

Who would not rejoice to place himself in the hands of such a Savior and Physician?

Answering forever the world's questions: "Is He able to heal? Does He ever heal? Does He always heal?"—to all we boldly say, "Yes, He is Jesus, triumphant, eternal, omnipotent."

Jesus called His twelve disciples and commanded upon them power and authority to cast out devils and heal disease.

(See Luke 9:1.) He superseded this by declaring: *"If ye shall ask **anything** in my name,…it shall be done"* (John 14:14, 15:7).

The first was a limited power of attorney; the second, unlimited. This unlimited power of attorney was authorized before His crucifixion. It was to become effective when the Holy Ghost came.

On the day of Pentecost this power of attorney was made fully operative. The Spirit came. First, legally, they had His Word. Then, vitally, He sent His Spirit.

Peter and John instantly grasped the significance of the name. Passing into the temple, they met a beggar-cripple. He was forty years old and had been crippled from birth. Peter commanded, *"In the name of Jesus Christ of Nazareth, rise up and walk"* (Acts 3:6). Heaven's lightning struck the man. He leaped to his feet, whole.

A multitude rushed up. They demanded, "In what name, by what power, have ye done this?" Peter and John replied, "In the name of Jesus Christ of Nazareth, whom ye slew, whom God raised up." (See Acts 3:12–16.) Matchless name! The secret of power was in it. When they used the name, power struck. The dynamite of heaven exploded.

Peter and John were hustled to jail. The church prayed for them in *"the name."* They were released. They went to the church. The entire church prayed that signs and wonders might be done. How did they pray? In *"the name."* They used it legally. The vital response was instantaneous. The place was shaken as by an earthquake. Tremendous name! (See Acts 3:1–16; 4:1–10, 23–31.)

Jesus commanded, *"Go ye into all the world"* (Mark 16:15). What for? To proclaim the name; to use the name; to baptize believers. How? In the name. Amazing name! In it was concentrated the combined authority resident in the Father, the Son, and the Holy Ghost. almighty name!

The apostles used the name. It worked. The deacons at Samaria used the name. The fire flashed. Believers everywhere, forever, were commanded to use it. The name detonated round the world.

More Bibles are sold today than any other 100 books. Why? The name is in it. It's finality—*"at the name of Jesus every knee* [shall] *bow…and every tongue* [shall] *confess"* (Philippians 2:10–11).

Prayer in this name gets answers. The Moravians prayed, and the greatest revival till that time hit the world. Finney prayed, and America rocked with the power. Hudson Taylor prayed, and China's Inland Mission was born. Evan Roberts prayed for seven years, and the Welsh revival resulted.

An old Negro, Seymour of Azusa, prayed five hours a day for three-and-a-half years. He prayed seven hours a day for two-and-a-half years more. Heaven's fire fell over the world, and the most extensive revival of real religion in this century resulted.

> *He said unto them, Go ye into all the world, and preach the gospel to every creature. He that believeth and is baptized shall be saved; but he that believeth not shall be damned. And these signs shall follow them that believe; In my name shall they cast out devils; they shall speak with new tongues; they shall take up serpents; and if they drink any deadly thing, it shall not hurt them; they shall lay hands on the sick, and they shall recover.*
>
> (Mark 16:15–18)

And lest healing should be lost to the church, He perpetuated it forever as one of the nine gifts of the Holy Ghost.

*To one is given by the Spirit the word of wisdom; to another the word of knowledge by the same Spirit; to another faith by the same Spirit; to another **the gifts of healing** by the same Spirit; to another the working of miracles; to another prophecy; to another discerning of spirits; to another divers kinds of tongues; to another the interpretation of tongues.* (1 Corinthians 12:8–10)

The church was commanded to practice it.

Is any among you afflicted? let him pray. Is any merry? let him sing psalms. Is any sick among you? let him call for the elders of the church; and let them pray over him, anointing him with oil in the name of the Lord: and the prayer of faith shall save the sick, and the Lord shall raise him up; and if he hath committed sins, they shall be forgiven him. Confess your faults one to another, and pray one for another, that ye may be healed. The effectual fervent prayer of a righteous man availeth much. (James 5:13–16)

The unchangeableness of God's eternal purpose is thereby demonstrated: "*Jesus Christ the same yesterday, and to day, and for ever*" (Hebrews 13:8), and "*I am the LORD, I change not*" (Malachi 3:6).

God always was the Healer. He is the Healer still and will ever remain the Healer. Healing is for you. Jesus healed all who came to Him. (See, for example, Matthew 8:36; 9:35; 12:15; Luke 4:40; 6:19.) He never turned anyone away. He never said, "It is not God's will to heal you," or that it was better for the individual to remain sick or that they were being perfected in character through the sickness. He healed them all, thereby demonstrating forever God's unchangeable will concerning sickness and healing.

Have you need of healing? Pray to God in the name of Jesus Christ to remove the diseases. Command it to leave, as you would sin. Assert your divine authority and refuse to have it. Jesus purchased your freedom from sickness as He purchased your freedom from sin.

> *His own self bare our sins in his own body on the tree, that we, being dead to sins, should live unto righteousness: by whose stripes ye were healed.* (1 Peter 2:24)

Therefore, mankind has a right to health, as he has a right to deliverance from sin. If you do not have it, it is because you are being cheated out of your inheritance. It belongs to you. In the name of Jesus Christ, go after it and get it.

If your faith is weak, call for those who believe and to whom the prayer of faith and the ministry of healing have been committed.

Chapter 5

Sin in the Flesh

Sermon

I want to bring you tonight a message taken from the eighth chapter of Romans. I will read you the first verses:

*There is therefore now no condemnation to them which are in Christ Jesus, who walk not after the flesh, but after the Spirit. For the law of the Spirit of life in Christ Jesus hath made me free from the law of sin and death. For what the law could not do, in that it was weak through the flesh, God sending his own Son in the likeness of sinful flesh, **and for sin, condemned sin in the flesh.***

(Romans 8:1–3)

For a long time I wondered what these two expressions meant: *"sin in the flesh"* and in the second verse, *"For the law of the Spirit of life in Christ Jesus hath made me free from the law of sin and death."* And then what it meant about that God *"condemned sin in the flesh."*

In the first place, we know that the physical body does not commit sin. (See 1 Corinthians 6:18–20.) It may be the

85

instrument or weapon that does the thing, but there is no sin in the physical body itself. Sin lies in the will. If you choose to sin, then you can make your body do it. Now according to law, there isn't any sin except it is performed by a physical act. You can think murder as much as you are a mind to, yet you are not a murderer in the sight of the law because you thought it. If you speak murder, that lays you liable, but the law recognizes nothing that has not been translated into conduct, into an act.

Now there isn't any sin in your physical body; there is nothing wrong with your body. Your body is all right. It is you, the hidden man of the heart, that makes the body do things that are unseemly and are wrong. (See Matthew 15:16–20.) Then what does He mean by sin in the flesh? For a long time that bothered me. I think I have found a key to it in the eleventh verse of this chapter, because it is all one argument.

> But if the Spirit of him that raised up Jesus from the dead dwell in you, he that raised up Christ from the dead shall also quicken your mortal bodies by his Spirit that dwelleth in you. (Romans 8:11)

Paul is not talking about the resurrection. He is talking about giving life, healing life, to our physical bodies. Our physical bodies don't need life unless they are sick, do they? That is the conclusion of the argument of Romans 8:1–11; that is a progressive single argument. What is he talking about? He is talking about disease and sickness and the sin that is in the flesh is the sin of a broken law in your body.

Now sin is breaking the law, some kind of law, and sin in the body is breaking a law of the body. Disease then is dis-ease, isn't it? Make it two words—dis-ease, broken law, wrecked ease, ease that has been destroyed. Ease is health. Dis-ease is sickness.

There are three kinds of sickness: sickness in the body, sickness in the soul, and sickness in the spirit. The basic sickness is spirit sickness. I venture this: If you could be healed in your spirit, every last one of you would be well in your bodies. But the whole problem is cleaning a man up in his spirit. Let me change it to business. If you can become a successful salesman in the spirit, you will put your bodies over.

Do you know the place you are whipped first is not in your mind, not in your body? You say, "Oh, my body is so tired." Your body is tired the moment that the spirit is discouraged. Your body breaks down under it. As long as your spirit is triumphant, you are a victor and go right on. A man is defeated only when he is defeated in his spirit. Let a man lose courage—and courage is not a product of the intellect— when he loses courage, he is whipped, and the only way to put the man on his feet again is to renew a right spirit within him. That isn't the Holy Spirit; it is to renew the spirit that has been defeated and conquered, whipped.

Healing then is in three planes, isn't it? Spirit healing, soul healing, and body healing. Basically, the person who is sick in body has likely been sick in spirit quite a little while, and after a while it has gotten down into the soul and passed through that into the body.

I cannot tell you, brethren, what this truth I am telling you now has meant to my life. I now can trace every physical change in my body to a spiritual condition. My body responds to my spirit.

Now, beloved, I want to give you something that is of infinite value just to illustrate it: I was called to a home to see a man of 82 or 83 years of age, day before yesterday. He has been sick now two years. He had blood poisoning in his teeth, and it went through his whole body. And when a man is past 80, it is bad, you know. I went into his presence with a well spirit, a conquering spirit. Now I didn't think of this when I went there.

When I went back today, I saw the effect. I was there with a triumphant, victorious spirit. His spirit caught the contagion from me. He was whipped. He had sat there in that chair until he was whipped, just defeated. Well, I sat down by his side and began to open the Scriptures, and something in me—and this is perfectly scriptural because out from your inner life, that is, your spirit, that is the inner being, shall flow rivers of living water—out from my spirit went into his spirit healing for his spirit. I didn't see it because he is a Scotchman, very reticent, didn't respond much. But I knew in me that it had gone into him. I knew that.

I talked to him a little while and opened the Word, and then prayed for him and left. This afternoon his beautiful, lovely, motherly wife, a woman along in years, called me up and said, "He wants to see you again. He is going to come down to the hotel to see you, because he doesn't think it is right to ask you to come way up here." Think of that, will you?

I said, "No, I will go up."

When I went into his presence this afternoon, I carried into his presence—I discovered it in myself immediately after I left the house—that I had carried into his presence health in my own mind. In my spirit I had carried a dominating, victorious spirit, and that man responded to it. Do you know what happened? Before I left the house, I saw the reactions in his physical body. Things had happened in his body. While I sat there and prayed for him, his spirit had become adjusted; the spirit in me received its health from the Lord, and I communicated something to his spirit, and his spirit made contact. Just as you press the button and turn on light, you make contact with God's Spirit, and when it did, healing came down into his body. Why, he changed his whole outward demeanor, changed everything about himself.

I have been defeated, and I am full of defeat; and that corroding defeat has come down over me, and I have lost out; I have broken connection. Did you ever see a battery in an auto corroded with something, and it had eaten off the wires, and the starter didn't move? What is the matter? Something corroded there. You should have kept that clean.

Corroding cares come and get in around your spirit life, and they just cover you and break your connection with the Lord. This is true. The real first healing is the healing of your spirit, getting your spirit adjusted to the Lord. The spirit is the part that contacts the Lord. If the spirit is out of harmony and out of condition, and is sort of broken down, you can't get faith for healing, can you? No, you must become adjusted to the Lord.

I said to a young man a little while ago—he was in a desperate condition, required a first-class miracle to touch his life at all—I sat by his side and said, "If you will accept Jesus Christ as your Savior and confess Him as your Lord, and you receive eternal life, you are healed."

He said, "What do you mean?"

I said, "Just the moment you are born again, you are healed." I have never been afraid to promise that to any unsaved person. Why, I didn't know that for years. Now I can tell you—it's the simplest thing in the world—the moment you are born again, eternal life comes into your spirit. That spirit then can come into the closest relationship with the

Father, the great Healer, and the life of God then pours down into his spirit and soul, into his body, and he is immediately touched and made whole.

You cannot get healing for the body, as far as you are personally concerned; *somebody else's faith may*, but until your spirit is right, you cannot get healing for your body. May I call your attention to another thing? Faith is a product of your spirit, not of your intellect. Your intellect does not produce faith. Your knowledge may give you grounds for faith, but faith is resident in your spirit.

Joy is something in your spirit. Happiness is something connected with your surroundings. You are happy because of your surroundings. You are joyful because you are in right relation with the Father. Now faith, love, joy, hope—all spring from your spirit being, the hidden man of the heart. All are products of your spiritual life.

The reason people do not have rich, beautiful faith is because their spirits are denied the privilege of communion and fellowship with the Father. You understand me? You don't read your Bible; you don't pour over it; you don't live in it; you don't spend any time in fellowship with the Father. Consequently, your spirit is depleted and weakened. Faith springs out of it, and the faith that grows out of it is a sickly plant.

On the other hand, your spirit life is fruitful and built up and enriched by communion with the Father and by reading His Word. And your spirit becomes strong and vigorous. There issues from it a faith that is triumphant and creative. I venture to say this: The men and women who are weak in faith, who once were mighty in faith, are so because they have stopped feeding on the Word of God and stopped close, intimate fellowship with the Father.

Let me say to you with all frankness, brother, that you cannot lose your faith until you have broken your fellowship. Just as long as your fellowship is rich and your spiritual life is at floodtide, faith is triumphant. I have followed that in my own life. For years I did not understand the law that governs it. I see it now. You see, here is the thing that is mightily important—that the spirit life in man is kept healthy and vigorous, and it is kept healthy and vigorous by three exercises. There are more ways, but three in particular.

One is *feeding on the Word*. Second is a *continual public confession* of what you are and what Jesus is to you. I am not talking of sin; I mean confession of your faith in Christ, of what Christ is to you, of His fullness, His completeness, and His redemption. And the third thing is *communion with Him*—feeding on the Word, confession, and communion. Three simple things, aren't they? And yet they are the things that produce great spiritual life. You do not have it without them.

There are three planes of healing: spiritual, mental, and physical. Now just for a bit, I want to call your attention to another very important fact: the relation of your body to your spiritual life. Paul said, in the ninth chapter of 1 Corinthians, that he kept his body under [subjection], lest haplessly after he preached to others, he himself would be laid aside (see verse 27)—not lost, but laid aside, no longer usable. Why? Because his body had gained the ascendancy over his spiritual life. If you become a glutton, and just live to gratify your appetite by eating and drinking, you will lose out spiritually. But if you will keep your appetite and your body under control like Paul says he did, your spirit will have a chance to evidence itself.

Now let me state it again. You may be a great spiritual athlete, or you may have been a great spiritual athlete, but somewhere you have stopped feeding on the Word. The Word lost its taste and flavor for you. You say, "How can it be?" It is. I know of preacher after preacher that had great power at one time, but they have lost all joy in the Scripture. How do I know? Well, I know by the way they act. When a man loves a woman, he wants her with him, doesn't he? He doesn't care to go off and spend evenings alone. And when a man loves his Bible, you will find the Bible with him, in his arms, somewhere. He has gotten hold of the thing. He is holding it.

When I find a man along in years and his hair is growing gray, and I find he loves his Bible, I know that man is fresh in his spirit life. One of the mightiest men I ever fellowshipped with in my life in prayer—when he and I would be together in prayer, sometimes I would open my eyes and look at him, and he would be on his knees with his Bible and kissing it. Didn't want anyone to see him. Thought my eyes were closed. He was holding it just as a man holds his wife in his arms and kisses and embraces her, kisses and loves her.

Whenever I reach a place where I lose my appetite for the Book, and rather talk with people than read the Bible, or rather read books about the Bible than to read the Bible, then I know I am backslidden in my spirit.

You can trace the downfall of every spiritual giant that I have ever known in my life to these three things. One of the greatest men this country ever produced—I have heard him when the Book was in his hand—when he preached like this, he drove me to my knees. Every time I would hear him, I would go out and get alone and pray if I could possibly do it. He just battered me and hammered me and drove me into my hole, so to speak; or else he filled me and thrilled me and lifted me.

I saw him twenty years later, when his name was in the lips of every man, and I heard him preach. I noticed that he quoted a good many Scriptures, but he never picked up his Bible; and I noticed he had a theory and philosophy of redemption instead of the old-time simple exposition of the Word. And I saw that man, whose name was known in every part of the world, with something like sixty churches in back of him, in a building that seated 3,500, and the building was not half full. He had the greatest gospel soloist that this country has ever produced, but the meeting was dry and dead as any formal set vice imaginable. They utterly failed.

I said to the singer, who left that field and came with me for a campaign or two, "Charley, what is the matter with him?"

"Well," he said, "I do not know, but he is no more like the man he used to be than anything in the world." There had no sin come into that man's life; his life was just as clean as it had ever been. But here is how it had come: Somehow or other he had broken in his spiritual life with the food of the Spirit, the Bible. And the second thing, he used to have the most marvelous prayer life, but he didn't have it anymore. And the third thing, in that whole sermon, I didn't hear one personal confession because he was preaching in a place where personal confession was taboo and people criticized it. If you said anything about yourself and your own experience, right off the ministers would say, "He is bragging about his own life, isn't he?"

Brother, you will brag about your own life if you have power with God, and you can't help this bragging; you have something to brag about. You really have. You walk in the fullness of the life and fellowship of your spirit with His

Spirit, and you have something to talk about, haven't you? Fresh new experiences are coming into you all the time. You are walking in the realm of miracles. I knew that man when he walked in the creative realm of faith. I knew him when he moved down into the purely intellectual realm.

Healing is basically a spiritual thing. The power that heals the sick comes down from God through your spirit, out through your hands, and into that man or woman. And if you are having the right kind of spiritual fellowship, you will have power with God, and there is no escaping it. But listen, brother, you can't get a powerful current of divine life from a little impoverished wire, can you? And you can't get it when the wire where it connects with you is corroded with worldly cares. Now we call in the electrician and say to him, "I want you to wire my spirit up with God. I want fresh equipment all the way through." Hallelujah!

You say, "I will tell you what I want. I want to be able to stand about 10,000 volts. I want to be wired up to God so that the fullness of His power can pour down through me, through my soul, and out through my hands and voice to the people."

How does that come to you? It is the simplest thing in the world. Your spirit interlocks with His Spirit without any foreign substance intervening. One day my Reo car stopped right in traffic. A young lady sat with Mrs. Lake and said, "Let me try it."

She worked the accelerator, and it wouldn't work. She said, "Wait a moment." I jumped out of the car and raised the hood. She said, "I can tell you where it is." She just opened up the distributor, and she said, "One of those points has got a fleck of dirt on it." She brushed it off with her handkerchief and put in on again. The car started right off. That point of the distributor had some little dust, something under it, some little corroding some way that just broke the current; and it was a delicate little thing—it didn't take much.

It doesn't take much to break the connection of your spirit and His. God is a Spirit. You are a spirit. And when something breaks the connection, the power no longer flows through. You say you want me to pray for you, and I pray for you. There is no power. What is the matter? Something has broken the connection. The power comes down through the one who prays, but it can't get through your spirit and touch you. Or, there may be something in my spirit, and His Spirit wants to communicate with your spirit, but is hindered by something in my spirit. But suppose you and I are both right in our spirits. You will get your healing as sure as God sits on His throne.

"But if the Spirit of him that raised up Jesus from the dead dwell in you, he that raised up Christ from the dead" (Romans 8:11) shall send healing through your spirit into your mortal flesh as sure as God is on His throne.

The second thing that must be done continually is, after you have fed on the Word and your spirit is open to the truth of confession, you can't bottle God up. You can't lock Him up. It has been God's method throughout all the ages to speak to people through those who are in right relation with Himself; and when you are in right relation with Him, the most normal and natural thing is that He will use you to communicate Himself to others. And so, you act as the medium through which He is to pour His message, by song or by testimony or by prayer or by some other means, but you are His medium. You are His testifier, His spokesman, His instrument through which He is going to work. Beautiful, isn't it?

Now, you see that keeps you in perfect communion, because you have to continually get new messages all the time from Him, so you live in perfect fellowship with Him, feeding on His Word and telling out the things He does for you. And no Christian is safe who hasn't a *now* experience with the Lord, because sickness can come on you and you have no power to throw it off. You have your *now* experience in your spirit, and you are continually in contact. The spiritual power is coming down and going back and forth continually. Things are coming down, and things are going up, from Him to you and you to Him, down through your spirit. You have a beautiful picture. Angels ascending and descending. It is the thoughts of God coming down and your thoughts going back—He feeding on you and you feeding on Him.

Now, the relation of your body to your spiritual life is almost an unexplored tableland of possibilities. Paul said, "Let not sin therefore reign as god in your death-doomed body." (See Romans 6:12.) Let not sin reign. What is sin? It is disease; it is dis-ease. He is not talking about sin, because if there is any sin in you, it is not in your body. If there is any sin, it is in your spirit or in your soul, isn't it? It is somewhere active in your thinking processes. But he says, "Let not sin reign as god in that death-doomed body." Sin is a broken physical law in your body, and that is sickness.

I have a boil, and the boil gains dominion and runs my body, my mind, and my spirit. All I do is to nurse that miserable, throbbing, aching enemy that is in there, raising the devil. That is sin in my flesh, and sin has been condemned in the flesh. God condemned the thing, and now sin has broken out in there.

What is rheumatism? Sin in the flesh. And sin shall not have dominion over you in your body for you are no longer under law, but under grace (see Romans 6:14) when your body has become the temple of God. Know ye not your body has become a member of Christ? Shall a member of Christ be made the member of a harlot? (See 1 Corinthians 6:15–16.) That does not necessarily mean a woman who is a harlot as we commonly use the word. It may be money, it may be gluttony, it may be a thousand things; but I have taken my body away from the Lord and the Lord's use, and I have committed it to some other use that should not be. *"Let not sin reign in your mortal body as king."* Hallelujah! *"Neither yield ye your members as weapons of unrighteousness"* (Romans 6:13). You turn your body over to be used by doctors to make money from, and surgeons chop you up for a splendid fee.

A woman said to me recently, "My daughter has determined that she will have an operation."

I said, "What is the matter with her?"

"The doctor doesn't know, but he thinks he ought to explore in there." Did you ever hear of it? And so he is going to cut her open and send a Livingstone in there to explore. Great, isn't it? Then the daughter will go—after she is all wrecked and ruined and she can't get any healing—then she will turn to the Lord. Then she will expect to get her healing without asking the Lord's forgiveness for turning her body over to some man for examination and experimentation. *"Know ye not that your body is the temple of the Holy Ghost?"* (1 Corinthians 6:19). Shall I take the temple of God, then, and turn it over to idols and to demons?

That body of yours is God's holy house, God's holy dwelling place. Why, it is the most sacred thing on earth. Now, the temple that God designed and gave to Israel in the wilderness contained the Holy of Holies, the inner place, didn't it?

And in the temple that Solomon was permitted to build for God was the Holy of Holies, for the Shekinah presence dwelt there. The Shekinah presence now dwells in your body.

Can you imagine, brethren, a beautiful church that cost half a million dollars? Everything is in perfect harmony: wonderful carpets and rugs, wonderful furniture, wonderful decorations, and the most up-to-date lighting scheme; everything is perfectly beautiful and artistic. It is just a dream of architectural beauty. They dedicate it to the Lord and go home. They dedicate it on Saturday. Sunday they are going to hold their first services in it, and when they open the door, they make the most awful discovery—a horrible stench rushes out to meet them. What has happened? I will tell you. A sacrilegious man opened the door last night and drove a herd of hogs into the sanctuary, and the hogs have been staying in the beautiful edifice during the night.

That is just what we do with these bodies of ours. We have dedicated them to God, and then we let a flock of unclean thoughts come in; we let disease come in and settle in our bodies until these precious bodies that belong to God are filled with the children of these unclean things. Tuberculosis is the child of a thought; it is the product of a mental and spiritual condition. This is true, that when we are in right communion and fellowship with the Lord, there is not power enough in all hell to put disease upon your little finger.

And we have permitted that flock of that dirty, devilish herd of swine to come into our bodies and fill them with disease.

Now beloved, let us go into the thing a little bit further. Then the real healing of your life begins in your spirit, doesn't it?

*Wherefore he is able also to save [heal] them to the ut-
termost that come unto God by him, seeing he ever liveth
to make intercession for them.*   (Hebrews 7:25)

Now brethren, if God is able to heal to the uttermost,
then there are no healings that are impossible, are there?
Absolutely none. It doesn't make any difference how sick
you are, there is healing for you if you are in contact with
the Healer. I don't care how beautiful your chandeliers are, I
don't care how beautiful your fixtures are—if outside, one of
the fuses blown out, you won't get any light. And the fuse that
lets the light of God into you is your spirit, and if that thing is
diseased and weak and sickly, you can't get much of a current
through it, can you?

A man had a vision. He saw a strange sight. He saw a
piece of desert land and sickly flowers and trees growing on
it. And he awakened and the picture persisted in following
him. The next night, he had the same picture come before
him again, and it persisted for three nights. Then he said,
"Lord, what is this?"

And a voice answered, "Don't you know what it is?"

And he said, "No, Lord, I don't know that I do." He sat
looking carefully at it again, and he could see it, oh, so vividly.
He said, "Lord, that is me, myself." And he said, "That desert is myself." And he said, "I can see the faith and love and
peace and joy that should grow there are those weak, sickly
plants."

The Lord said, "What would you do if your garden was
like that?"

He said, "I'd hoe it and cultivate it and irrigate it." And
the Lord left him to think it over.

Now, if your faith is weak and sickly, it is because your spiritual connection with the Lord is faulty. Maybe there is a fuse blown. Maybe a switch is out. But there it is. Now, there must be a right adjustment of the soul to the body and of soul and body and spirit. I am a threefold being, if I want to put it that way. To get the highest results, my spirit must be dominant. My soul must be subservient to my spirit. My body must be under control of my soul. Then when my body and soul and spirit are in rapport, when they are in perfect fellowship with each other, they can bring forth real results, can't they?

"Know ye not that your body is the temple of the Holy Ghost?" (1 Corinthians 6:19). Now when that comes to pass, then there come two spirits. There are two spirits in your body now; there was one before. It was a renewed spirit; then the great, mighty Holy Spirit came in. Now you have two spirits in your body and one soul.

Now the Holy Spirit wants to dominate your spirit, and He wants, through your spirit, to communicate the unveilings of the Father through the Word to your intellect and bring your intellect and your affections up into perfect harmony with His will. And you yield yourself to Him, and you pour over the Book and take it as your own. You read it, you feed upon it, you eat it—it is more necessary than your daily food. *"Man shall not live by bread alone, but by every word that proceedeth out of the mouth of God"* (Matthew 4:4). And you pour over the Word and you meditate on it, and you get at the heart of the thing, and your spiritual nature grows and develops until it dominates your intellect. But you just read intellectual things, read novels and cheap stories, and your sickly intellect will absolutely dominate your whole life and break your communion with the Lord and leave your spirit life in darkness.

The way to health is back again to where we belong, isn't it? I venture this: It is possible to rebuild your spiritual life, just as you can rebuild a broken body. I have told you how many of the great athletes grow strong. One of them I met years ago was given up to die of tuberculosis. Another of the great athletes, one of the great wrestlers, was given over to die of tuberculosis at eighteen. He became one of the outstanding wrestlers in America. What a man can do in his physical body he can do in his spirit, and it can be done with his intellect. There is absolutely no reason why our spiritual lives should not be up to 100 percent efficiency.

I wish I was keen enough in my spiritual nature; I'd have a blackboard put behind us, and I'd have someone come who understood artwork. I would look over the audience, and I'd take each one of them, and I'd say to the artist, "Draw that man's spirit and let me show his spiritual condition," and you would see your spirit up there. If it was a weak, sickly, puny thing, you would see it.

Do you know some folks—if you could see them when they come into the meeting, their spirits are on stretchers, emaciated, tubercular, no flesh on them, just skinny, horrible-looking living corpses? They have great big husky bodies, but their spirits are shrinking, feeble, emaciated things. And they come up and say, "What is the matter with me? I don't seem to have any joy with the Lord." Well, a tubercular spirit will have no special joy. "I know I have spiritual discernment." Imagine! I say, "Brother, you have spiritual tuberculosis. Your spirit is emaciated. I don't know whether it will survive the night."

Another comes to me and says, "What is the matter with me?"

I look at him carefully for a moment. "Do you want me to diagnose it?"

"Yes, sir."

"You have cancer, yes, sir. It is on your spirit, it is laying siege to the jugular vein of your spirit, and I don't think it will be but a little while before it will finish off your spiritual life. It will kill you outright."

Another man says, "I will tell you what ails me." He said, "I will illustrate it. My little boy used to take his money to buy his lunch at school. Instead of buying lunch, he bought candy and cheap soda water to drink, and he ate pie and cake and candy until by and by we found out." The man said, "I found out he would not eat meat, and he wouldn't eat vegetables, and we thought there was something desperately wrong with him, and there was. So we just put a spy on his track, and we found out he was buying candy and eating it." Aha.

Now, if your spirit has reached the place where it has no appetite for the things of God, you have been playing hooky. You have been feeding on things that you ought not to eat, and you have compelled your poor spirit to feed on trash and cheap scandal and cheap talk and useless talk, wisecracking and everything, and you have never given your spirit any real healthy food for a long time, and the poor thing is dying of hunger.

Do you understand me now? You can't get your [physical] healing until you get your spiritual healing. If you get your healing, you will get it through the doctor's faith, don't you see? And you will lose it again. But if you get it through your own spirit being in perfect fellowship with the Lord and somebody praying for you likely, or you praying for yourself, or else nobody praying for you, you will be able to keep it.

The doctor told of an experience he had down in Texas where a whole congregation had come, practically all of them for healing, and he said, "You just sit here and listen to me preach, and I won't pray for you at all." He said the largest percentage of the congregation was perfectly healed in just a little while. They came every day for thirty days. At the end of the thirty days, there was only about 7 percent of the whole congregation that was not healed. All they did was get spiritually healed; and when you get spiritually healed, chances are a hundred to one that you will be healed physically.

And I want to tell you this—I don't want to hurt your feelings, God bless you, but brother, do you know I have discovered this?—there are quite a number of folks that come to be prayed for, and they are healed over and over again. The healing you need is not physical but spiritual. You get right and get adjusted so you are feeding on the Word, and so you are giving public testimony, and you will be well or in a condition to get well.

Chapter 6

The Power of Divine Healing

~~◆~~

Sermon

My soul used to be able to enjoy as much lightness in the Lord Jesus as anybody, but various processes of life reduced my capacity to enjoy jingle, and God brought me down into the solids of life. No man could live in the environment in which a large portion of my life has been spent, without realizing that unless men can contact the living God in *real power*, power out of the ordinary, power sufficient for tremendous needs and unusual occasions, he could not live. Man could not live!

In South Africa some years ago, in a single night, a fever epidemic struck the country for three hundred and fifty miles. As I rode through a section of that country, I found men dead in their beds beside their wives, children dead in their beds alongside the living, whole families stricken, dying, and some dead. In one single month, one-fourth of the entire population of that district, both white and black, died. We had to organize an army to dig graves, and an army of men to make caskets. We could not buy wood enough in that section of the country to make caskets, so we buried them in blankets—or without when it was necessary to save the blankets for a better purpose.

I had a man in my company who perhaps some of you know. God had appointed that man to pray as I have never found anybody else anointed to pray. For days he remained under a thorn tree, and when I passed that way in the morning, I would hear his voice in prayer; and when I returned in the evening, I would hear his voice in prayer. Many times I got a prepared meal and carried it to him and aroused him long enough to get him to eat it. I would say, "Brother, how is it? Are you getting through?"

He would reply, "Not yet." But one day he said, "Mr. Lake, I feel today that if I had just a little help in my faith, that my spirit would go through into God." And I went on my knees beside him, joined my heart with his, and voiced my prayer to God.

As we prayed, the Spirit of the Lord overshadowed our souls, and presently I found myself not kneeling under the tree, but moving gradually away from the tree some fifty or one hundred feet. My eyes gradually opened, and I witnessed such a scene as I had never witnessed before—a multitude of demons, like a flock of sheep. The Spirit had come upon him also, and he rushed ahead of me, cursing that army of demons, and they were driven back to hell or to the place from whence they came. Beloved, the next morning when we awoke, that epidemic of fever was gone. *That is the power of divine healing*—God destroying Satan.

Now when you consider that I have been a man of some scientific training, you can understand what an introduction into a life where everything was made new and of a different order meant. Instead of being on the hard, natural plane of materialistic life and knowledge, suddenly introduced into the Spirit, you can realize what a revolution was brought to pass in my soul and how gradually discovery after discovery revealed the wonder of God and the mighty action of God through the souls of men.

There is a little keynote in one of Paul's epistles that gives the real key to successful prayer. In successful prayer there is a divine action, a divine interaction, an interaction just as real as any chemical interaction in any experiment in the world. You bring two opposite chemicals together, and you realize a little flash or flame, an explosion. There has been an interaction; your chemicals have undergone a change. They are no longer the same properties they were before.

For instance, oxygen and hydrogen unite in water. So it is in the spiritual realm. Paul said in giving us this key: *"The word preached did not profit them, not being mixed with faith"* (Hebrews 4:2). There is a quality and content in the soul of man, a necessary quality. That quality is the *power of the Spirit.* And when faith and Spirit come together, there is an interaction. There is a movement of God. There is a manifestation of the Spirit. There is a divine explosion! *Faith and God united* **is** *divine healing!*

When I was a boy, a neighbor employed a chemist. They were trying to manufacture a new explosive of some kind. A section of the barn was being used for the experiments. Johnnie was strictly reminded that he had no business around the barn, but like many Johnnies, his curiosity was aroused. One day when they had gone to town, he discovered that the door was not thoroughly locked. Just a little picking and prying and it opened, and Johnnie was inside. There were some packages on the bench and some liquid on the floor. Presently, Johnnie bungled; a package fell into a bucket of liquid and that is the last Johnnie remembered. When he came to himself, he was some fifty or seventy feet away, and they told me he was carried there by a section of the wall. It just went off. That package and the liquid interacted.

We look at the wonderful powers in nature and marvel. Not long ago, a group of scientists compressed such a quantity of nitrogen in a solid block thirteen inches square that they declared if it would be placed in the heart of the city of Chicago and permitted to explode, it would wreck the city. One can imagine somewhat of the terrific energy stored up in that little block of nitrogen thirteen inches square; and when you come to think of the marvel of the nature of God, the dynamic of His being—how staggering His almightiness becomes!

The world's conception of religion is that it is a matter of sentiment. In the minds of most men, religion is just sentiment to them; it is not a thing of power. They do not understand the properties of the soul of God, nor the quality of His life, nor how it is that God moves in the nature of men to change their hearts, to dissolve the sin out of their souls, to cleanse them by His life and power, to heal their bodies, and to reveal His light and life in them.

I believe the very beautiful thing we call *salvation* and the holy statement of Jesus Christ, "*Ye must be born again*" (John 3:7), is itself a scientific fact and declaration of God's divine purpose and intent, based on the law of being. We are inclined to think that God just desires, and our hearts are changed. But I want to tell you, beloved, that there is a process in a man's soul that admits God into his life. Your heart opens because it is touched by the love of God; and into the heart, into the nature of man, there comes the divine essence of the Living Spirit; and bless God, it has an action in him. Sin dissolves from his nature and from the mind of man. The Spirit of God takes possession of the cells of his brain, and his thoughts are changed by its action. There is a new realization of divine holiness. By the grace of God, he discovers himself sanctified in deed and in truth because Christ in truth dwells there.

Beloved, Jesus Christ had His eye and His soul fixed on that one dynamic power of God—the Holy Ghost. And His holy life, His death, His resurrection, His ascension to glory were all necessary in the process of soul development to arrive at the throne of God, where He could receive from the Father the gift of the Holy Ghost and have the privilege of ministering to your soul and mine.

So in my heart, there has grown a wondrous reverence for the mighty Son of God, who saw beyond the ken[4] of man; who envisioned in the distance; who sought in His soul for the key to the mighty powers of the nature of God; who determined for our relief and for our benefit and salvation to leave the throne of God, come to earth, be born as a man, and take upon Him the nature of man (not the nature of angels). He looked to God as men do, overcome by His power. Through reliance on His Word and so believing, so advancing step-by-step in the nature of God and the likeness of God, one day He stood forth, the Eternal Sacrifice before the throne of God and received the eternal reward of His fidelity—the Holy Ghost. In life, Jesus the man was in the *likeness* of God; in resurrection, the *nature* of God; in glorification, the *substance* of God; and thus became the author of eternal salvation.

The man or the woman who does not understand the Holy Ghost and its magnificence and the wonder of its power,

---

[4] *ken*: the range of perception, understanding, or knowledge. *Merriam-Webster's 11th Collegiate Dictionary* CD-ROM, © 2003.

must turn his heart again heavenward and see the price that Jesus paid in order to secure it for you and me. In order to give it to the world that was in sin, sickness, and death—to lift it out of darkness. I love that blessed old hymn, "Ye Must Be Born Again." Can we not sing it?

> A ruler once came to Jesus by night,
>   To ask Him the way of salvation and light;
> The Master made answer in words true and plain;
>   "Ye must be born again!"
>
> Chorus: "Ye must be born again!"
>   "Ye must be born again!"
> "I verily, verily say unto thee,
>   'Ye must be born again!'"
>
> Ye children of men, attend to the Word,
>   So solemnly uttered by Jesus the Lord.
> And let not this message to you be in vain,
>   "Ye must be born again!"
>
> O ye who would enter this glorious rest,
>   And sing with the ransomed the son of the blest;
> The life everlasting if ye would obtain,
>   "Ye must be born again!"
>
> A dear one in heaven thy heart yearns to see,
>   At the beautiful gate may be waiting for thee;
> Then first to the note of his solemn refrain:
>   "Ye must be born again!"

There is a process of divine *transmutation*. But beloved, by the power of God's Spirit in a man's heart, that process is going on every single day of your life. God takes that which is natural, that which is earthly, touches it by His divine power, moves upon it by His heavenly nature, and in the name of

Jesus Christ you come forth no longer self and selfish, but now *transformed*, changed by the power of Christ, into the nature of the Son of God, into the likeness of the Lord, into His character and nature and understanding and knowledge. Blessed be the God and Father of our Lord and Savior Jesus Christ!

"To us is given exceeding great and precious promises, that by these ye may be partakers of the divine nature," and being a partaker, in consequence, escape *"the corruption that is in the world through lust"* (2 Peter 1:4). Bless God, His divine purpose is not to whitewash the soul but to change the character, transmute the life by the grace of God, make the man a priest and king, a deliverer and a savior in common with the Lord Jesus Christ, his Elder Brother. If I am a brother of the Lord, then I am bone of His bone and flesh of His flesh and substance of His substance, just like my Elder Brother. The source of life is the same source of life that is in Him. The same purpose that is revealed in Him is His high purpose for you and for me.

Men have little understanding of the quality of faith or what it accomplishes, because of the fact that they are not aware of the process by which that work is done. Faith has the quality and power, with the Spirit of God, to do what a match does to powder. It is the touch of God. It is the touch of faith through us that ignites the Spirit and produces the divine action that takes place in the soul when sin is rebuked and cast out, when sickness is destroyed and dissolved from the life, the nature set free, and man rejoices as a son of God, saved in spirit, soul, and body.

One day there came to my healing rooms a little boy that we know on the streets as a newsboy, just one of the little ragged chaps. A lady had observed the little fellow on the street in an epileptic fit and afterwards took him by the hand

and led him into the healing rooms. We talked to the little chap about the Lord, prayed for him, and told him to return again. The Lord healed him. He was a manly little urchin, and one day he said, "Mr. Lake, I haven't any money to reward you with now, but you are not going to lose any money on me." We smiled and were glad to see the spirit of the little chap, and he went his way. About two weeks later, in the midst of a great meeting, he strutted in, marched up, and laid five silver dollars on the table and marched out again.

Then he got up against his first real problem of living his new life in his business. Every boy has a corner. He can sell papers on his own corner, and it is up to him to keep all the other boys away. He had given his heart to the Lord. One day he came around with a long face. He said, "It's all off."

"Well, my boy, what's the trouble?"

"They were going to rush my corner, until I could not stand it, and I cleaned up the whole bunch." The little chap was getting his first introduction into the real problem of being a Christian in this old world, under a competitive system, the outgrowth of human selfishness, devised by the devil.

One day, a gentleman came along and wanted to buy a paper, but his arm was disabled, and he could not get his purse. He said to the boy, "I have put my purse in the wrong pocket. Put your hand in and get it for me."

The boy said, "What is the matter with your arm?"

He replied, "I have what is called neuritis. My arm is paralyzed."

The little chap said, "Well, if the doctors can't do you any good, I'll tell you where you can get it fixed up. There are some men up in the Rookery Building who pray, and folks get well."

The man said, "How do you know?"

He replied, "I used to take fits and fall on the street, and they would carry me off to the police station. I was like that for four years, but I don't take fits any more. If you want me to, I will take you up there." So he brought him up.

The man was the head of a great lumber concern; his name was Rose. He sat down and told me how he was moved by the child's simple words, but he had no idea of how God could heal a man or save man from sin. So we began to tell of the Lord Jesus and His power to save and continued to minister to him each day. Three weeks afterward, he returned again to the medical clinic where two hundred and seventy-five physicians had declared four weeks before that they could do nothing for him. They reexamined him and found him perfectly well, healed by the power of God. *That is the power of divine healing.*

I went to the medical association and got a copy of the lecture that was given by Dr. Semple on the seriousness of the disease and the utter impossibility of medicine ever to help him or change his condition. Insofar as they were concerned, he was a cripple. The nerves were dead, atrophied. It would require a miracle, they said, to reproduce the original life and restore power in the tissue of the arm. But the miracle took place because there is a fountain of life, the life of God, available for every man. Bless His name! *That is the power of divine healing.*

When the *life* of Jesus comes in, the death of your soul ends. When the Spirit of God comes in, your *dead* nerves come alive; God, by the Spirit, takes possession of the blood and the brain and the bone. He dwells in the very cellular structure of your whole being. His quickening *life* regenerates you, and generates life in you, and by the Christ of God you come forth, not a dead, senseless lobster, but a *living man,* a *living* Christian.

Let me tell you a story to illustrate this point. They say a man died, and he appeared at the Beautiful Gate and said to Peter, "I am from Philadelphia. I subscribe to the *Ladies' Home Journal*. I have a bed of mint in the backyard, but I never drink intoxicants."

Peter replied, "Go on to heaven and *stay dead*." He was dead already. Some folks think, you know, that because they are not committing this sin or that sin that they are dutiful, beautiful children of God. But, beloved, there is an awful lot more to Christianity than delivering a man's soul from the power of sin.

Professor Riddell tells this story:

> I was walking along the Sea Beach, and I encoun-
> tered a lobster. I said, "Lobster, did you ever chew
> tobacco?"
> "Never!"
> "Lobster, did you ever stay out nights?"
> "Never!"
> "Say, Lobster, shake hands. We are both lobsters."

Oh, there is a negative thing, and that negative thing in religious life is what is killing the real power of God. That negative thing is when we all the time are *not doing* this and that and something else. It is a religion of *don't* do this, and *don't* do that. My God! When Christ comes into the soul and into the spirit, it is all changed. Instead of deadness, there is *life* in God. Instead of inaction, there is *power* by the Spirit of God. The Christian is a *man*, not a lobster.

Down in the human heart,
  Crushed by the tempter,
Feelings lie buried

That grace can restore.
Touched by a loving heart,
  Wakened by kindness,
Chords that were broken
  Will vibrate once more.

Oh, the grace of God is the lovely thing; the grace of God
is the powerful thing. The grace of God is the life and Spirit of
the Lord and Savior Jesus Christ. And ministered to the soul,
breathed into the heart, transmitted to the life, *man* becomes
like Christ because the Christ of God is moving in the heart
of him, generating and regenerating; and man comes forth a
finished product by the hands of his Lord—saved from sin,
healed of disease, kept by the indwelling Christ, who is the
power of God.

I am looking to God for some real finished products these
days, real men grown up in the Lord Jesus Christ, established
in the splendid solidarity of His holy nature and divine character, beautified by His holy glory, enriched by His divine
nature—like *the Son of God*.

So, my brother, my sister, I want to bring your hearts
this afternoon into this blessed confidence, this holy truth,
this divine reality. If religious life has been a sort of sentiment, let me tell you that, beyond it, there is the power of
God. The moving, dynamic, burning force of life in Christ
Jesus is waiting to come into your heart, to revitalize your
thought, and to change your spirit and indwell the very flesh
and bone and blood of you and make you a new man and a
new woman in the Lord Jesus. Beloved, *that is the power of
divine healing*.

On one occasion, I was entertaining myself by examin-
ing some typhoid bacteria as they developed in dirty water. A

neighbor woman came one morning and was anxious for me to show her one of her hairs under the microscope. I told her I had the microscope set and was waiting for the development of the bacteria and would be obliged if she would come back another day, when my experiment was over. Instead of paying attention to what I said, she returned the next day with the same request. Again I explained to her, but the next morning she was back again, and finally the fourth morning. I was annoyed and thought I would just take one of her hairs, let her see it anyway and not disturb the microscope. So I pulled it through under the microscope and let her look. Presently, she jumped up and hurried away and never even said, "Thank you."

When I came home that evening, Mrs. Lake said, "What did you do to Mrs. B?"

I said, "I really do not know. Why?"

She said, "Well, she has been on the back porch all day, and the servant has been drenching her hair with kerosene. Why, she saw more crawling things than she ever saw before." She had seen the bacteria and believed the crawling beasts were attached to her hair. Her hair and head were perfectly clean. The presence of the beasts she saw was explained in another way.

I want to bring home the truth of God. In the minds and lives of many, religion is simply an illusion. There is no divine reality in it. But, beloved, real religion is God's divine reality, for it is the heart of God and the life of Christ. And when it comes into the soul of man, it generates the same divine reality and heavenly power in him, and man becomes God's new creature.

Chapter 7

Divine Healing

❦

Sermon · Dutch Church Hall
Somerset East, South Africa · October 1910

Beloved, I feel a personal responsibility in speaking to you on the subject of divine healing. This truth was very little known and still less understood prior to the arrival of Brother Tom Hezmalhalch and myself upon these shores, in connection with the introduction and the establishment of the Apostolic Faith Mission in this land.

We had prayerfully considered this subject on our way from America to this country, and had come to the decision that the present was an opportune time to separate this truth from the dogmas and traditions which bound it, and to send it forth on broader lines in harmony with our conception of the truth as it is revealed to us in the Scriptures.

You will therefore appreciate my feelings as I undertake to address you tonight on this subject.

It is affirmed by the thoughtless that we teach new doctrines. It is not so, for...

Divine Healing Is Not New

It has come to us through a process of progressive revelation running parallel with man's history and perfected in the vicarious death and suffering of our Lord on Calvary.

In its stages of evolution and development, it finds its illustration and parallel in the baptism of the Holy Ghost, which advances from a revelation from God to man in the patriarchal age to that of God dwelling and abiding with man in the Mosaic age, and reaches its climax in the baptism of the Holy Ghost in the Christian dispensation—which is God in man, whereby man becomes the habitation of God through the Spirit.

In Exodus 15:26, God revealed Himself to the people of Israel under His covenant name of *Jehovah-Rophi*, or *"the* LORD *that healeth thee."*

There at the waters of Marah, after they had escaped from the Egyptians and Egyptian medical practitioners by crossing the Red Sea, God made with them…

An Everlasting Covenant

There he made for them a statute and an ordinance, and there he proved them, and said, if thou wilt diligently hearken to the voice of the LORD *thy God, and wilt do that which is right in his sight, and wilt give ear to his commandments, and keep all his statutes, I will put none of these diseases upon thee, which I have brought upon the Egyptians: for I am the* LORD *that healeth thee.*
(Exodus 15:25–26)

The covenants of God are as unchangeable and eternal as Himself. The covenant of divine healing stands today as steadfast and irrevocable as the day it was made by the eternal, immutable God at the waters of Marah. It is writ large upon the pages of Holy Writ. Saints have rejoiced in it; prophets have confirmed it; David, the sweet psalmist of Israel, sang in inspired verse of its validity:

> *Bless the Lord, O my soul: and all that is within me, bless his holy name. Bless the Lord, O my soul, and forget not all his benefits; who forgiveth all thine iniquities; who healeth all thy diseases.* (Psalm 103:1–3)

Jesus Christ, who was God manifest in the flesh, demonstrated the perpetuity of that covenant in Himself, *"healing all manner of sickness and all manner of disease among the people"* (Matthew 4:23); by communicating the power of healing the sick to all believers (see Mark 16:15–17); and through the Holy Ghost, placing *"the gifts of healing"* (1 Corinthians 12:9) as a perpetual manifestation of His power and presence in the church through all ages.

Jesus Christ, like any great reformer, had a specific mission to fulfill. This was outlined in the inspired words of the prophet Isaiah. (See Isaiah 61:1–2.) In the synagogue at Nazareth, at the beginning of His public ministry, Jesus announced the essential points embraced in that ministry imposed upon Him, and which He said was now being fulfilled. Healing was one of the conspicuous features of that ministry, as we read in the fourth chapter of Luke:

> *The Spirit of the Lord is upon me, because he hath anointed me to preach the gospel to the poor; he hath sent me to heal the brokenhearted, to preach deliverance to the captives, and recovering of sight to the blind, to set at liberty them that are bruised, to preach the acceptable year of the Lord.* (Luke 4:18–19)

Like a true reformer and the Son of God, He put His mission into immediate effect and practice. How did He do it? Read the fourth chapter of Matthew, and you will see the evolution of the ministry of healing:

> *And Jesus went about all Galilee, teaching in their syna-gogues, and preaching the gospel of the kingdom, and healing all manner of sickness and all manner of disease among the people.* (Matthew 4:23)

In the ninth chapter of Luke, we read of the first step taken by our Lord suggestive of the broadening, progressive scope of this ministry of healing, by sending forth...

Twelve Other Men with Power to Heal

> *Then he called his twelve disciples together, and gave them power and authority over all devils, and to cure diseases. And he sent them to preach the kingdom of God, and to heal the sick.* (Luke 9:1–2)

And He said unto them, "Take a thousand pounds a year." Is that it? [Voices: No!] Then what is it?

> *And he said unto them, take nothing for your journey, neither staves, not scrip, neither bread, neither money; neither have two coats apiece.* (verse 3)

Oh, my! That is not much like your modern preachers! Today it means the finest house in town, the highest salary, the smartest carriage and horses! Everybody bows down before this display of so much worldly pomp and temporal greatness! These are some of the reasons why the church has lost spiritual power and stands impotent in the presence of sickness and suffering. To hide her feebleness and inefficiency, she takes refuge under the discreditable subterfuge that the gifts of healing have been withdrawn and the age of miracles is past. No wonder infidelity is eating the heart out of the church of God! Has *Jehovah-Rophi*, the eternal covenant God, changed? Or, is the modern disciple of a different stamp and pattern than they whom Jesus called in the days of His flesh? Truly, the change is in the disciple and not in the one unchangeable Lord and Master. I find that the old-time power is to be had today by the old-time men who are willing to walk and work and suffer and die to get this gospel of Christ to people everywhere.

He endued the twelve with the power. And in the tenth chapter of Luke we read how the Lord took an additional step to the extension of the scope of the ministry of divine healing by sending forth...

Seventy More Men with the Power to Heal

"*After these things the Lord appointed other seventy also*" (Luke 10:1); and in verse 9 we read that Jesus commanded them to "*heal the sick that are therein, and say unto them, the kingdom of God is come nigh unto you.*" There were now eighty-three men endued with this power: Christ Himself, the twelve disciples, and the seventy more. At the close of the forty days separating the event of the crucifixion from that of the ascension, our Lord still further extends the range of the ministry of healing by furnishing...

Every Believer with the Power to Heal the Sick

Every person, in every age, in every land, who has faith in the living, eternal, covenant-keeping God is empowered to lay hands upon the sick, and "*they shall recover*" (Mark 16:18). The general terms of that great extension of the ministry of healing are found in that great and final commission given in Matthew 28: *"And Jesus came and spake unto them, saying, all power is given unto me in heaven and in earth"* (verse 18).

Beloved, has He lost any of that power? Never! He is still the Son of God.

> *All power is given unto me in heaven and in earth. Go ye therefore, and teach all nations, baptizing them in the name of the Father, and of the Son, and of the Holy Ghost: teaching them to observe all things whatsoever I have commanded you: and, lo, I am with you alway, even unto the end of the world.* (Matthew 28:18–20)

Is He with us still? Yes, bless God. Is He changed? No. *"Jesus Christ the same yesterday, and to day, and for ever"* (Hebrews 13:8). *"I am the* LORD, *I change not"* (Malachi 3:6). *"For the gifts and calling of God are without repentance"* (Romans 11:29). God has never repented of having placed the gifts of the Holy Ghost in the church. In the name of Jesus Christ, I challenge any man to show by the Word of God that the gifts and power of God were withdrawn. We have lost the old-time faith—that is where the trouble is! Having forsaken God to lean upon the arms of flesh, and the fountain of living waters for broken cisterns that can hold no water (see Jeremiah 2:13), let us honestly acknowledge our sin and return to the Lord our God.

Having examined the general terms of that extension of the ministry of healing, let us now consider the peculiar characteristic, the trademark of God's endorsement, which was to be the accompanying circumstance, the continuous sign and symbol of the gospel of Jesus Christ.

This is given in the sixteenth chapter of Mark:

> *Afterward he appeared unto the eleven as they sat at meat, and upbraided them with their unbelief and hardness of heart, because they believed not them which had seen him after he was risen. And he said unto them, Go ye into all the world, and preach the gospel to every creature. He that believeth and is baptized shall be saved; but he that believeth not shall be damned. And these signs shall follow them that believe; in my name shall they cast out devils; they shall speak with new tongues; they shall take up serpents; and if they drink any deadly thing, it shall not hurt them; they shall lay hands on the sick, and they shall recover.* (Mark 16:14–18)

"And these signs." These are God's own mark and endorsement of the faithful preaching of the gospel of Jesus Christ. We know the goods by the trademark that they beat. These signs are God's eternal trademark, issued by the Son of God, and sealed in His own blood. The devil has tried to rob us of it by telling the preachers and teachers that these verses are an interpolation, and not found in the Sinaitic manuscript of the New Testament.[5] The Sinaitic manuscript was, however, only written in the fourth century. That these verses are authentic has been proved from the writings of the church fathers, which were written prior to the Sinaitic manuscript, and less than two hundred and seventy years after Christ.

This is a matter of history. Lord Hailes, an eighteenth century Scottish writer, is our authority. He tells us that at

---

[5] The Sinaitic manuscript, one of the most prominent discovered after 1611, was found amongst trash paper in St. Catherine's monastery at the foot of Mt. Sinai in 1841. It is considered a flawed manuscript.

a dinner at Edinburgh, it was decided that a compilation of the New Testament be made from the New Testament references and quotations found in the writings of the church fathers, previous to AD 300. The whole was completed some years ago and found identical with our present edition, except that it lacked seven verses in Hebrews, and these have since been forthcoming. Preachers and teachers of God's Word, don't make any more infidels with such an excuse, but rather confess that the faith to get results is lacking, that the Word is true, that the failure is on the human side.

Have you noticed how frequently church officers and members say, "Oh, I don't believe this or that portion of God's Word!" Why don't they? How could they when the Word of God is continually twisted out of its original sense and meaning by those whose vocation should be to guard it as a sacred deposit? This wresting of the Scriptures is responsible for the unwarranted belief that the gifts of the Holy Ghost have been withdrawn.

Jesus said, *"These signs shall follow* [not the doubter, but] *them that believe; in my name* [the name of Jesus] *shall they cast out devils; they shall speak with new tongues; they shall take up serpents; and if they drink any deadly thing, it shall not hurt them; they shall lay hands on the sick, and they shall recover."*

Someone asks, "What does it mean to cast out devils?" It means that the man with the Holy Ghost dwelling within him is the master and has dominion over every devilish force and counterfeit. At Johannesburg, someone said, "Your power is hypnotism." One night, God demonstrated through us the falsity of that accusation. The power that is within the true Christian is the power of the living Christ, and *"greater is he that is in you, than he that is in the world"* (1 John 4:4).

I can best illustrate this by introducing an incident in my own personal ministry.

The Power of God against Hypnotism

In the Johannesburg Tabernacle, at a Sunday evening service about a year ago, God instantly healed a lame girl. She came from Germiston. She had been suffering for three-and-a-half years from what the doctors said was either an extreme case of rheumatism or the first stage of hip disease. She was not able to get up the steps without assistance when she came to the platform to be prayed for. They asked her, "How long have you been sick?"

She said, "For three-and-a-half years."

"Have the doctors treated you?"

"Yes; for two-and-a-half years, and then they gave me up."

"Who has been treating you for the last year?"

"A hypnotist."

Just then, a well-known hypnotist arose in the audience and moved forward and took the front seat. The leader said, "Never mind about the hypnotist; Jesus is going to heal you right now. In two minutes you will be well." They laid hands on her and prayed, and instantly the Lord delivered her, and she walked up and down the platform several times to demonstrate to herself and the audience that she was well.

The leader said:

I stepped back and looked at her, my heart going out in praise to God for His mercy, when suddenly the Spirit of the Lord descended upon me in power—not in any gentle influence, but with a mighty intense power—a spirit of revulsion against the spirit in the hypnotist. I stepped on the platform directly in front of him and said, "Are you the man who has been hypnotizing this woman?"

He replied, "Yes, I am." He rose to his feet and looked towards me in a challenging attitude.

I said to him, "In the name of Jesus Christ, you will never hypnotize anybody again." And before I realized what I was doing, I reached over the front of the platform, grasped his collar with my left hand, while with my right I slapped him on the back, saying, "In the name of Jesus Christ, the Son of God, you come out of him. Now," I said, "go and hypnotize another if you can."

He laughed at me and said, "Do you mean to tell me that I cannot hypnotize anybody?"

I said, "Yes, sir, that is the end of the thing. The devil that caused you to hypnotize people is out."

He worked all night in an endeavor to hypnotize some subjects, and in the morning at six came to my house saying, "This is a mighty serious business, mister, this is my bread and butter." He wanted me to give him back the power to hypnotize.

I explained to him that it was not I but Jesus who had cast out the devil. I added, "Brother, it looks to me as if the Lord wanted you to earn an honest living."

He cancelled his engagement at the theatre where he was billed to give exhibitions, and last heard of, he was working in the mine and earning an honest living.

That demonstrated there is a mighty manifestation of the Spirit of God that has dominion over every other power. It is still true that in His name we shall cast out devils.

Brother Fisher and "They Shall Take Up Serpents"

This afternoon I heard a brother ask, "What about *'They shall take up serpents'?*" Let me tell you a story. Brother Fisher of Los Angeles, California, told me this incident in his own life. He was a Baptist minister at Glendale, a suburb of Los Angeles. (He is now associated with Brother George G. Studd in the Upper Room Mission, 327½ South Spring Street, Los Angeles, California, USA.)

> One morning my wife called me up on the telephone and said the water pipe beneath the house was broken. I went home about ten in the morning. I opened the little door in the basement of the house and, on putting my hand in to feel for the pipe, I was bitten by a serpent. At once I commenced to swell. The poison worked into my body fast. What was I to do? I said, "God, Your Word says, 'They shall take up serpents.' I trust You for this; You must heal me or I die."
>
> That afternoon and evening my sufferings were terrible. By midnight my blood was so congealed I was well nigh insensible. Oh, I shall never forget that sense of death creeping over me, steadily, surely, until three in the morning. I could pray no more. I ceased to struggle, I fell to the floor, and that instant God healed me. The life of God thrilled through my body, and I was healed. It is true, "They shall take up serpents."

Brother Tom and "They Shall Take Up Serpents"

Let me give you another illustration of "taking up serpents." It is an event in the life of Brother Tom Hezmalhalch, one of the pastors of the Apostolic Faith Mission in Johannesburg. Brother Tom, as we call him for short, is a man of great faith and simple trust in God. (He has since returned to America.)

> In Southern California, during one of the harvest seasons, I had an honest young infidel working for me. The young man was engaged in loading, and I was pitching sheaves on the load, when he said, "Brother Tom, do you believe in the Bible?"
>
> I said, "Every word of it."
>
> He said, "Do you believe in Mark 16:18?"
>
> I said, "I do."
>
> He answered, "I have never yet met the person who does."
>
> I prayed silently to Jesus, that if He wanted to convince this young man of the truth of His Word, that He send along a snake, and I would take it up. Soon I heard a hissing sound from under the sheaves. I said, "Jesus sent you along; I want you." I grabbed the snake some distance from the head, and I lifted it up to my friend on the wagon. He looked at me and then said, "Kill it! Kill it!"
>
> "No," I said, "Jesus sent it along; I am going to let it go about its own business."
>
> After a while he laughed, and said, "Tom, that was only a common Californian snake."
>
> I judged from his expression he was not satisfied with the test. I prayed again. "Jesus, why did You

send along a common snake? If you want to convince this man, send along a venomous one."

Not long after, I heard the hiss of another snake. I cried, "Hold on there; I want you," and laying hold of it as I did the former one, I held it up to my friend, saying, "How about Mark 16:18?"

He turned pale and said hastily, "Drop it! Drop it! Kill it."

I put it quietly down after stroking its head and body with my other hand, and said, "Go on, Jesus sent you here, I'll not kill you."

When my friend could speak, for he was pale and shocked, he said, "Tom, did you know what kind of a snake that was?"

I said, "No."

He replied, "That was a deadly viper, and if it had bitten you, you would be a dead man."

I said, "It could not bite. Jesus would not permit it."

I don't pretend to have that kind of faith, but I am not going to belittle it in the man who has. I am, I trust, man and Christian enough to praise God when I see someone going further than I can.

"If They Drink Any Deadly Thing, It Shall Not Hurt Them"

You ask, "What about, 'If they drink any deadly thing, it shall not hurt them'?" History abounds with instances in which the early Christians were compelled to drink the juice of the deadly hemlock, but through faith in Jesus, one of the deadliest of poisons became as harmless as water. According to your faith be it done unto you. (See Matthew 9:29.)

My own sister's son, Fred Moffatt, when a child, entered his father's workshop and ate some Paris green.[6] My sister and brother-in-law sent for me. I quoted the words of our Savior, *"And if they drink any deadly thing, it shall not hurt them."* Upon this precious promise of God we rested, and Jesus healed the child. (His parents now reside at 4 Milbourn Road, Bertrams, Johannesburg, and their son was a student at the Marist Brothers Schools and has since returned to America.)

I have outlined the development and progressive revelation of divine healing from the covenant at Marah, and on through succeeding dispensations until it is perfected in the redemption wrought by Christ on Calvary. The blessings of healing in the old as well as the new dispensation flow from the atonement that Jesus Christ, the Son of God, made for man's sin and sickness on the cross of Calvary.

In Matthew, we read:

> *He cast out the spirits with his word, and healed all that were sick: that it might be fulfilled which was spoken by Esaias the prophet, saying, Himself took our infirmities, and bare our sicknesses.* (Matthew 8:16–17)

In the general epistle of James, through the inspired writer, the Holy Ghost instructs the Christian what to do when sick.

> *Is any sick among you? Let him call for the elders of the church; and let them pray over him, anointing him with oil in the name of the Lord: and the prayer of faith shall save the sick, and the Lord shall raise him up; and if he hath committed sins, they shall be forgiven him.* (James 5:14–15)

---

[6] *Paris green*: a very poisonous emerald green copper and arsenic compound used especially formerly as an insecticide and pigment. *Merriam-Webster's 11th Collegiate Dictionary* CD-ROM, © 2003.

In spite of the clear, convincing testimony of the Scriptures and the ever accumulating cloud of witnesses who testify of healing received through faith in Jesus, many preachers and teachers are still found blindly rejecting the truth to their own final discomfiture and undoing.

God Has a Controversy with the Church in Africa

Your own prophet, the Reverend Andrew Murray, was healed of God at Bethshan, London, England, of a throat disease that medical skill had proved itself impotent to heal. Thirty years ago the reverend gentleman wrote a book containing the fundamental teaching on divine healing. Why was it withdrawn from circulation? Why is it not possible to obtain this book at any of the Christian literature depots in Africa?

Why? Because the preachers foresaw that the members of their churches would call upon them for the exercise of that faith which saves the sick! They feared the ordeal which would test their faith in God and the value of their own prayers! Instead of confessing their spiritual poverty and inefficiency and reaching out to touch the springs of life and power in God, they fell back into a state of even greater spiritual apathy and inertness, being satisfied with the cold externals of religious forms and observances, which without the indwelling life-giving power and presence of the Holy Ghost have no saving grace or spiritual virtue.

Divine Healing Is the Seal of God's Acknowledgment

Divine healing is the seal of God's acknowledgment and the proof to the world that Jesus Christ is the Son of God. John the Baptist was in prison. He was troubled with doubts as to whether Jesus was the Christ. He sent two of his disciples to Jesus to put the question, *"Art thou he that should come, or do we look for another?"* (Matthew 11:3). Jesus' answer was to appeal to the signs of His ministry. These were, and are still, God's answer to doubt or unbelief:

> Go and show John again these things which ye do hear and see: The blind receive their sight, and the lame walk, and the lepers are cleansed, and the deaf hear, the dead are raised up, and the poor have the gospel preached to them. And blessed is he, whosoever shall not be offended in me. (Matthew 11:4–6)

These are still God's seal and endorsement of the preaching of the true gospel. The preaching that lacks the signs that Jesus promised lacks the divine attestation by which God confirms the preaching of as own true gospel. *"Take heed, brethren, lest there be in any of you an evil heart of unbelief, in departing from the living God"* (Hebrews 3:12).

And at the end of the age as at the beginning, the command of Jesus Christ to all workers everywhere is:

> Go ye into all the world, and preach the gospel to every creature. He that believeth and is baptized shall be saved; but he that believeth not shall be damned. And these signs shall follow them that believe; In my name shall they cast out devils; they shall speak with new tongues; they shall take up serpents; and if they drink any deadly thing, it shall not hurt them; they shall lay hands on the sick, and they shall recover. (Mark 16:15–18)

The results now, as then, will be, *"And they went forth, and preached every where, the Lord working with them, and confirming the word with signs following"* (Mark 16:20).

"My Grace Is Sufficient for Thee"

The other evening I was riding home after a heavy day's work; I felt very wearied, and sore depressed, when swiftly, and suddenly as a lightning flash, that text came to me: *"My grace is sufficient for thee"* (2 Corinthians 12:9). I reached home and looked it up in the original, and at last it came to me in this way: *"My grace is sufficient for thee."* I said, "I should think it is, Lord," and burst out laughing. I never fully understood what the holy laughter of Abraham was until then. It seemed to make unbelief so absurd. It was as though some little fish, being very thirsty, was troubled about drinking the river dry, and Father Thames said, "Drink away, little fish, my stream is sufficient for thee."

Or, it seemed like a little mouse in the granaries of Egypt, after the seven years of plenty, fearing it might die of famine. Joseph might say, "Cheer up, little mouse, my granaries are sufficient for thee." Again, I imagined a man away up yonder, in a lofty mountain, saying to himself, "I breathe so many cubic feet of air every year; I fear I shall exhaust the oxygen in the atmosphere." But the earth might say, "Breathe away, O man, and fill thy lungs ever, my atmosphere is sufficient for thee." Oh, brethren, be great believers! Little faith will bring your souls to heaven, but great faith will bring heaven to your souls."

—Charles H. Spurgeon

They shall be abundantly satisfied with the fatness of thy house; and thou shalt make them drink of the river of thy pleasures. (Psalm 36:8)

> *I am come that they might have life, and that they might have it more abundantly.* (John 10:10)

> *But my God shall supply all your need, according to his riches in glory by Christ Jesus.* (Philippians 4:19)

Jehovah fills to the brim the vessels faith presents to Him.

The present circumstance, which presses so hard against you, if surrendered to Christ, is the shaped tool in the Father's hand to chisel you for eternity. Trust Him then. Do not push away the instrument lest you lose its work.

A Nickel for the Lord

Yesterday he wore a rose on the lapel of his coat, but when the plate was passed today, he gave a nickel to the Lord. He had several bills in his pocket and sundry change, perhaps a dollar's worth, but he hunted about, and finding this poor little nickel, he laid it on the plate to aid the church militant in its fight against the world, the flesh, and the devil. His silk hat was beneath the seat, and his gloves and cane were beside it, and the nickel was on the plate—a whole nickel.

On Saturday afternoon he met a friend, and together they had some refreshments. The cash register stamped thirty-five cents on the slip the boy presented to him. Peeling off a bill he handed it to the lad and gave him a nickel tip when he brought back the change. A nickel for the Lord and a nickel for the waiter.

And the man had his shoes polished on Saturday afternoon and handed out a dime without a murmur. He had a shave and paid fifteen cents with equal alacrity. He took a box of candies home to his wife and paid forty cents for them, and the box was tied with a dainty bit of ribbon. Yes, and he also gave a nickel to the Lord.

Who is this Lord? Who is He? Why, the man worships Him as Creator of the universe, the One who puts the stars in order, and by whose immutable decree the heavens stand. Yes, he does, and he dropped a nickel in to support the church militant.

And what is the church militant?

The church militant is the church that represents upon the earth the triumphant church of the great God.

And the man knew that he was an atom in space, and he knew that the almighty was without limitations, and knowing this he put his hand in his pocket, and picked out the nickel, and gave it to the Lord.

And the Lord being gracious, and slow to anger, and knowing our frame, did not slay the man for the meanness of his offering but gives him this day his daily bread.

But the nickel was ashamed, if the man was not.

The nickel hid beneath a quarter that was given by a poor woman who washes for a living.

—G. F. Raymond, in the *Toronto Star*

Chapter 8

Letter to the Editor, *The Sun*

Letter · Addressed to Editor, *The Sun*

In appearing before the San Diego public at the Egyptian Tent Theatre Sunday, I do not come as a theorist but bring the richness and ripeness of thirty years of strenuous Christian life, such as few in our day have had opportunity to experience. In appealing to God alone and trusting Him only under almost every known circumstance, I have had abundant experience. I relate a few of these for the benefit of your readers.

In 1911, a scientific party was going into the depths of unexplored Africa. I begged to be permitted to accompany the party for the sake of companionship with white men. When in the depth of tropical African forest, the party was stricken with blackwater fever (malaria). Four of the seven died in five days, including the doctor and the surgeon; I was the only member of the party not sick. When it became known the surgeon was dead, the three dying men went into the blackness of despair; all were hopeless. I then told them

137

of my faith in Christ as the Healer as well as Savior of men, and begged them to let me minister to them and to trust Him for themselves as best they were able. I spent two days and three nights in fasting and prayer with them. They were healed, and we finished the trip without remedy or preventative medicine of any kind.

In 1908, a terrible epidemic of African fever struck the Zuitpansberg district. In one month, one-fourth of the entire population, both black and white, died. I was then in Zuitpansberg. In riding from home to home among the isolated Dutch Boers (farmers), I found on the fourth day of the epidemic, women dead in bed by their husbands and vice versa; children two and three in a bed, sometimes two dead; the whole family stricken, no one able to assist another.

I then rode seventy-five miles over the mountains to the neatest telegraph station and reported the situation to Louis Botha, then Premier of the Transvall. He wired me to remain on the job and represent the government until relieved and that forty ox wagons would leave Pretoria at four AM with supplies. An ox wagon has from sixteen to forty-eight oxen attached. When the situation at my missionary headquarters became known, four Europeans volunteered to come and assist me. I buried all four in three weeks and was left alone to do what I could. The government had reached us with medical assistance and a proper organization was set up. In this epidemic, I saw thousands healed through prayer only, both white and black. In this service, the Transvall Parliament gave me a vote of thanks.

I not only believe in healing of disease but believe that, through faith in God, we can be tendered virtually immune from disease and contagion.

In 1912, an epidemic of smallpox ran riot among the isolated Matabele natives; tens of thousands died. We were six hundred miles from civilization. Natives in this district wear no clothes. Imagine trying to lift a big, helpless native from a mat on the hut floor when his naked body is covered with eruptions that would burst under your hands and by the pressure on your body as you carried him about. Do it all day, and imagine the state of your clothes by night, when your overalls and jumper would be soaked through with smallpox pus. Then, having no change of clothes, you went to the nearest creek and washed them out as best you could and walked about in your birth clothes till they dried; then next day you did it over.

I have lived with and prayed for thousands of African lepers and, in all my African experience, never contracted disease or carried contagion to my family. It is because of such experiences as the above that I say I do not come to the people of San Diego with untried theories, but out of the strenuous past draw the lessons of faith in God that make life to him who has [been] hidden in Christ glorious and give to the soul of man the divine mastery.

—Dr. John Graham Lake

Chapter 9

An Address to the People of the Inland Empire

Sermon • By John G. Lake, Overseer

In the religious life, when one arises with a larger vision of God's purpose for mankind then that usually presented by religious teachers, his declarations are received with question. Men who think desire to be convinced by word, by the Holy Scriptures, and by demonstration, that the teacher's assertions at are not correct.

It was demanded of the prophets that the signs of a prophet should be seen.

Jesus never intended Christianity to be received and believed on any man's statement, *but provided* that the statement should be accompanied by an exhibition of spiritual power that would convince *the world*, saying to His followers:

> *These signs shall follow them that believe; In my name shall they [believers] cast out devils; they shall speak with new tongues;...they shall lay hands on the sick, and they shall recover.* (Mark 16:17–18)

This was Jesus' own test of the truth, but also a test of true discipleship.

The people demanded of Jesus, "What sign dost thou show?" (See John 2:18.) They challenged His authority to *forgive sins*, until convinced by His reasoning and the healing of the palsied man, of His authority and power. Jesus was a reasonable man; He was not only willing to discuss the issue with them, but to heal a man in their presence, as He did, saying:

> But that ye **may know** [be convinced] *that the Son of man hath power on earth to forgive sins...I say unto thee* [addressing the palsied man], *Arise, and take up thy bed, and go thy way into thine house. And immediately he arose, took up the bed, and went forth before them all.* (Mark 2:10–12)

This was a mark or brand by which the world might know an impostor and also recognize the true faith of Christ. Christianity was to be its own witness through its power to deliver from sin and heal from disease all who needed deliverance. (See Mark 16:17–18; John 5:13–15.)

Paul warned Timothy to beware of those who have a form of godliness but no power of God in their lives, saying, "*Having a form of godliness, but **denying the power thereof**: from such turn away*" (2 Timothy 3:5).

Paul further declared his own preaching was not based on men's wisdom, but was demonstrated by the power of God through him. He said:

> And my speech and my preaching was not with enticing words of man's wisdom, but in demonstration of the

> *Spirit and of power: that your faith should not stand in*
> *the wisdom of men, but in the power of God.*
> (1 Corinthians 2:4–5)

When Peter and John healed the lame man at the beautiful gate of the temple, the people demanded, "By **what power**, or by **what name**, *have ye done this?*" (Acts 4:7). And Peter replied:

> *Be it known unto you all, and to the people of Israel, that*
> *by the name of Jesus Christ of Nazareth, whom ye cruci-*
> *fied, whom God raised from the dead, even by him doth*
> *this man stand here before you whole.* (Acts 4:10)

Jesus gave a test of the character and quality of the Messenger and the power He exercised. He said, "*Ye shall know them by their fruits. Do men gather grapes of thorns, or figs of thistles?*" (Matthew 7:16).

We contend, by the Word of God, that the world and the church have been robbed of the presence, power, and blessing of Jesus Christ, a present Healer, because the church has falsely taught that the days of miracles are past. The days of miracles never passed, only in the soul that lost its faith in God. Where faith is, there ever will be the evidence of God's mighty power to save and heal.

Chapter 10

The Ministry of Healing and Miracles

❧❦❧

Sermon

Divine Healing Is Scientific

Atonement through the grace of God is scientific in its application. Jesus used many methods of healing the sick. All were scientific. Science is the discovery of how God does things.

Jesus laid His hands upon the sick in obedience to the law of contact and transmission. Contact of His hands with the sick one permitted the Spirit of God in Him to flow into the sick person.

The sick woman who touched His clothes found that the Spirit emanated from His person. She *"touched the hem of His garment,"* and the Spirit flashed into her. (See Matthew 9:20–22.) She was made whole. This is a scientific process.

Paul, knowing this law, laid his hands upon handkerchiefs and aprons. The Bible says that when they were laid upon the sick, they were healed, and the demons went out of those possessed. Materialists have said this was superstition. It is entirely scientific. The Spirit of God emanating from Paul transformed the handkerchiefs into "storage batteries" of Holy Spirit power. When they were laid upon the sick, they surcharged the body, and healing was the result. (See Acts 19:12.)

Firstly, this demonstrates that the Spirit of God is a tangible substance, a heavenly materiality. Secondly, it is capable of being stored in the substance of cloth, as demonstrated in the garments of Jesus or the handkerchiefs of Paul. Thirdly, it will transmit power from the handkerchiefs to the sick person. Fourthly, its action in the sick man was so powerful, the disease departed, and the demonized were also delivered. And fifthly, both the sick and the insane were delivered and healed by this method.

Men received Jesus Christ into their hearts as one receives a lover. It is an affectionate relationship. Men obey Him, because they have received Him affectionately. He has become their souls' lover.

His love and power in them redeems them from sin and sickness and eventually, we are promised in His Word, He will redeem us from death also. (See John 8:51–52; Romans 6:4–5, 8:2; 1 Corinthians 15:26, 54; 2 Timothy 1:10; Revelation 21:4.) Redemption from sin, sickness, and death constitutes man's deliverance from bondage to Satan and his kingdom and establishes the kingdom of heaven.

The Power of the Name

Jesus called His twelve disciples and commanded upon them power and authority to cast out devils and heal disease. (See Luke 9.) He superseded this by declaring, *"If ye shall ask anything in my name, I will do it"* (John 14:14).

The first was a limited "power of attorney." The second was unlimited. This unlimited "power of attorney" was authorized before His crucifixion. It was to become effective when the Holy Ghost came. (See Luke 24:49; Acts 1:8.)

On the day of Pentecost, this "power of attorney" was made fully operative. The Spirit came. (See Acts 2:2–43.) First, legally: they had His Word. Then, vitally: He sent His Spirit.

Peter and John instantly grasped the significance of His name. Passing into the temple, they met a beggar-cripple. He was forty years old and had been crippled from birth. Peter commanded, *"In the name of Jesus Christ of Nazareth rise up and walk"* (Acts 3:6). Heaven's lightning struck the man. He leaped to his feet, whole.

A multitude rushed up. They demanded, "In what name, by what name, by what power, have you done this?" (See Acts 4:7.) Peter and John replied, *"In the name of Jesus Christ of Nazareth, whom ye crucified, whom God raised from the dead"* (verse 10).

Matchless name! The secret of power was in it. When they used the name, power struck. The dynamite of heaven exploded.

Peter and John were hustled off to jail. The church prayed for them in *"the name."* They were released. They went to church. The entire church prayed that signs and wonders might be done. How did they pray? In *"the name."* They used it legally. The vital response was instantaneous. The place was shaken as by an earthquake. Tremendous name! (See Acts 4:3–31.)

Jesus commanded, *"Go ye into all the world"* (Mark 16:15). What for? To proclaim that name; to use that name; to baptize believers.

How? In the name (His authority; what He commanded). Amazing name! In it was concentrated the combined authority resident in the Father, the Son, and the Holy Ghost. almighty name!

The apostles used the name. It worked. The deacons at Samaria used the name. (See Acts 9:31.) The fire flashed. Believers everywhere, forever, were commanded to use it. The name detonated around the world.

More Bibles are sold today than any other 100 books. Why? The name is in it. It's finality: "At the name of Jesus, every knee shall bow and every tongue confess!" (See Philippians 2:10–11.)

Prayer in this name gets answers. The Moravians prayed. The greatest revival till that time hit the world.

The grace and love of God in the soul opens the nature to God. When they asked of the blind man, "What do you think of Him?" he replied, *"He is a prophet"* (John 9:17).

Later, Jesus found him and said to him, *"Dost thou believe on the Son of God?"* The man asked, *"Who is he, Lord, that I might believe on him?"* Jesus answered, *"It is he that talketh with thee"* (John 9:35–37).

The struggle of the centuries has been to free the soul from narrow interpretations. Jesus has sometimes been made to appear as a little bigot, sometimes as an impostor. The world is still waiting to see Him as He is: Jesus the magnificent, Jesus the giant, Jesus the compassionate, Jesus the dynamic—the wonder of the centuries.

Take the shackles off God.

Let Him have a chance to bless mankind without limitations.

As a missionary, I have seen the healing of thousands of heathen. Thus was Christ's love and compassion for a lost world revealed. And thus the writer was assisted into the larger vision of a world Redeemer whose hand and heart are extended to God's big world; and every man, saint and sinner, is invited to behold and love Him.

In one of the letters received from readers, this question is asked: "Why are not all persons healed instantly, as Jesus healed?"

The writer of this letter is mistaken in thinking that Jesus always healed instantly. A case in point is the healing of the ten lepers: *"As they went, they were cleansed"* (Luke 17:14). The healing virtue was administered. The healing process became evident later.

Again, Jesus laid His hands on a blind man and then inquired, "What do you see?" The man replied, *"I see men as trees, walking"* (Mark 8:23). His sight was still imperfect. Then Jesus laid His hands on him the second time, *"and he was restored and saw every man clearly"* (verse 25).

Healing is by degree, based on two conditions: first, the degree of healing virtue administered; and second, the degree of faith that gives action and power to the virtue administered.

> *The word preached did not profit them, not being mixed with faith in them that heard it.*   (Hebrews 4:2)

The miracles of Jesus have been the battleground of the centuries. Men have devoted their lives in an endeavor to break down faith in miracles. More believe in miracles today than ever before.

Pseudoscience declares miracles impossible. Yet the biggest men in the scientific world are believers in the supernatural and know that miracles are the discovery, the utilization of which the material scientist knows nothing.

The miracle realm is man's natural realm. He is by creation the companion of the miracle-working God. Sin dethroned man from the miracle-working realm, but through grace he is coming into his own.

It has been hard for us to grasp the principles of this life of faith. In the beginning, man's spirit was the dominant force in the world. When he sinned, his mind became dominant; sin dethroned the spirit and crowned the intellect. But grace is restoring the spirit to its place of dominion. When man comes to realize this, he will live in the realm of the supernatural without effort. No longer will faith be a struggle but a normal living in the realm of God. The spiritual realm places man where communion with God is a normal experience. Miracles are then his native breath.

No one knows to what extent the mind and the spirit can be developed. We have been slow to come to a realization that man is a spirit and his spirit nature is his basic nature. We have sought to educate him along intellectual lines, utterly ignoring the spiritual, so man has become a self-centered, self-seeking being.

Man has lost his sense of relationship and responsibility toward God and man. This makes him lawless. We cannot ignore the spiritual side of man without magnifying the intellectual and the physical. To do this without the restraint of the spirit is to unleash sin and give it dominance over the whole man. There must be a culture and development of the spiritual nature to a point where it can enjoy fellowship with the Father God. It is above mind, as God is above nature.

Man's intellect is ever conscious of supernatural forces that he cannot understand. He senses the spirit realm and longs for its freedom and creative power. But he cannot enter until changed from self and sin; the spirit must be enthroned and in action rather than the intellect—spirit above *both mind and matter.*

The life of God, the Spirit of God, the nature of God, are sufficient for every need of man. In the highest sense of the word, he is a *real* Christian whose *body, soul,* and *spirit* alike are filled with the life of God.

Healing in any department of the nature—whether spirit, soul, or body—is but a means to an end. The object of healing is health, abiding health of body, soul, and spirit. The healing of the spirit unites the spirit of man to God forever. The healing of the soul corrects psychological disorder and brings the soul processes into harmony with the mind of God. And the healing of the body completes the union of man with God when the Holy Spirit possesses all.

Is it true that today God is abandoning the *"virtue* [that] *went out of him and healed them all"* (Luke 6:19) for medical science? Would it not be abandoning the perfect for the imperfect?

Chapter 11

"Behold, I Give You Power"

Sermon

*When he was come down from the mountain, great
multitudes followed him. And, behold, there came a
leper and worshipped him, saying,
Lord, if thou wilt, thou canst make me clean.*
—Matthew 8:1–2

That man knew that Jesus had the power to heal him,
but he did not know it was God's will and that Jesus
had committed Himself to the healing of mankind.
If he had known, he would have said, "Lord, heal me."

It is always God's will to heal. Our faith may fail. My
faith failed to the extent that unless someone else had gone
under my life and prayed for me, I would have died. But God
was just as willing to heal me as He could be. It was my faith
that broke down. God is willing, just as willing to heal as He
is to save. Healing is a part of salvation. It is not separate from
salvation. Healing was purchased by the blood of Jesus. This
Book always connects salvation and healing. David said:

153

> *Bless the* LORD, *O my soul, and forget not all his benefits: who forgiveth all thine iniquities; who healeth all thy diseases.* (Psalm 103:2–3)

There never has been a man in the world who was converted and was sick at the same time, that might not have been healed if he had believed God for it. But he was not instructed in faith to believe God for healing.

Supposing two men came to the altar. One is sick and lame; the other is a sinner. Suppose they knelt at the altar together. The sinner says, "I want to find the Lord." All in the house will immediately lend the love of their hearts and the faith of their souls to help him touch God. But the lame fellow says, "I have a lame leg," or, "My spine is injured; I want healing." Instead of everybody lending their love and faith in the same way to the man, everybody puts up a question mark.

That comes because of the fact that we are instructed on the Word of God concerning the salvation of the soul, but our education concerning sickness and His desire and willingness to heal had been neglected. We have gone to the eighth or the tenth grade or the university on the subject of salvation, but on the subject of healing, we are in the ABC class.

> *Jesus put forth his hand, and touched him, saying, I will; be thou clean.* (Matthew 8:3)

Did He ever say anything in the world but "I will"? Did He ever say, "I cannot heal you because it is not the will of God" or "I cannot heal you because you are being purified by this sickness" or "I cannot heal you because you are glorifying God in this sickness"? There is no such instance in the Book.

On the other hand, we are told, "He healed *all* that came to Him." (See Matthew 4:24, 8:16, 12:15; Luke 4:40, 6:19.) Never a soul ever applied to God for salvation or healing that Jesus did not save and heal! Did you ever think of what calamity it might have been if a man had come to Jesus once and said, "Lord, save me," and the Lord had said, "No, I cannot save you"? Every man forevermore would have a question mark as to whether God would save him or not. There would not be universal confidence, as there is today.

Suppose Jesus had ever said to a sick man, "No, I cannot heal you." You would have the same doubt about healing. The world would have settled back and said, "Well, it may be God's will to heal that man or that woman, but I do not know whether it is His will to heal *me*."

Jesus Christ did not leave us in doubt about God's will, but when the church lost her faith in God, she began to teach people that maybe it was not God's will to heal them. So the church introduced the phrase, "If it be Thy will" concerning healing. But Jesus healed all who came to Him. (See Matthew 4:23; Luke 9:6, 11.)

Notice what it says in Isaiah:

*He will come and **save** you. **Then** the eyes of the blind shall be opened, and the ears of the deaf shall be unstopped. **Then** shall the lame man leap as an hart, and the tongue of the dumb sing.* (Isaiah 35:4–6)

Salvation and healing connected!

That it might be fulfilled which was spoken by Esaias the prophet, saying, Himself took our infirmities, and bare our sicknesses. (Matthew 8:17)

And lest we might be unmindful of that great fact that "*he hath borne our griefs* [sicknesses, infirmities] *and carried our sorrows*" (Isaiah 53:4), Peter emphasized it by saying,

> *Who his own self bare our sins in his own body on the tree, that we, being dead to sins, should live unto righteousness: by whose stripes ye were healed.*
>
> (1 Peter 2:24)

Not "by whose stripes ye *are* healed," but "*by whose stripes ye* **were** *healed.*" The only thing that is necessary is to *believe* God. God's mind never needs to act for a man's *salvation*. He gave the Lord and Savior Jesus Christ to die for you. God cannot go any farther in expressing His will in His desire to save man. The only thing that is necessary is to believe God. There is salvation by blood. There is salvation by power that actually comes from God into a man's life. The blood provided the power. Without the blood there would have been no power. Without the sacrifice there never would have been any glory. Salvation by blood, salvation by power.

The church in general is very clear in her faith on the subject of salvation through the sacrifice of the Lord and Savior Jesus Christ. Christians in general, regardless of their personal state of salvation, have a general faith and belief in the Lord and Savior Jesus Christ for the salvation of the world. But they are ever in doubt and very inexperienced on the power of God.

> *When he was come down from the mountain, great multitudes followed him. And, behold, there came a leper and worshipped him, saying, Lord, if thou wilt, thou canst make me clean. And Jesus put forth his hand, and touched him, saying, I will; be thou clean. And*

immediately his leprosy was cleansed. And Jesus saith
unto him, See thou tell no man; but go thy way, show
thyself to the priest, and offer the gift that Moses com-
manded, for a testimony unto them. (Matthew 8:1–4)

Did you ever stop to think that there is no medical remedy for the real things that kill folks? Typhoid fever: Fill the
patient with a tank full of medicine, and he will go right on
for twenty-one days.

In 1913, I was in Chicago in a big meeting, when I received a telegram from the hospital in Detroit, saying, "Your
son, Otto, is sick with typhoid fever. If you want to see him,
come." I rushed for a train, and when I arrived, I found him in
a ward. I told the man in charge I would like a private ward for
him, so I could get a chance to pray for him. Well, God smote
that thing in five minutes. I stayed with him for a couple of
days until he was up and walking around. He went along for
four or five weeks, and one day to my surprise, I got another
telegram telling me he had a relapse of typhoid.

So I went back again. This time there was no sunburst
of God like the first time. Everything was as cold as steel,
and my, I was so conscious of the power of the devil that I
could not pray audibly, but I sat down by his bed and shut my
teeth, and I said in my soul, "Now, Mr. Devil, go to it. You
kill him if you can." And I sat there five days and nights. He
did not get healing instantly the second time. It was healing
by process. Because of that fact, my soul took hold on God;
I sat with my teeth shut, and I never left his bedside until it
was done.

You may be healed like a sunburst of God today, and tomorrow, the next week, or the next month when you want
healing, you may have to take it on the slow process. The

action of God is not always the same, because the conditions are not always the same.

In the life of Jesus, people were instantly healed. I believe Jesus has such a supreme measure of the Spirit that when He put His hands on a man, he was filled and submerged in the Holy Ghost, and the diseases withered out and vanished.

But, beloved, you and I use the measure of the Spirit that we possess. (You can, as a member of His body, possess the Spirit in the same measure as He; God does not expect us to fulfill John 14:12 with less equipment than Jesus had.) And if we haven't got as much of God as Jesus had, then you pray for a man today, and you get a certain measure of healing, but he is not entirely well. The only thing to do is to pray for him tomorrow, and let him get some more, and keep on until he is well.

That is where people blunder. They will pray for a day or two, and then they quit. You pray and keep on day by day and minister to your sick until they are well. One of the things that has discredited healing is that evangelists will hold meetings, and hundreds of sick will come and be prayed for. In a great meeting like that, you get a chance to pray once and do not see them again. You pray for ten people, and as a rule, you will find that one or two or three are absolutely healed, but the other are only half-healed or quarter-healed or have only a little touch of healing.

It is just the same with salvation. You bring ten to the altar. One is saved and is clear in his soul. Another may come for a week, and another for a month, before they are clear in their souls. The difference is not with God. The difference is inside the man. His consciousness has not opened up to God.

Every law of the Spirit that applies to salvation applies to healing likewise.

And when Jesus was entered into Capernaum, there came unto him a centurion, beseeching him, and saying, Lord, my servant lieth at home sick of the palsy, grievously tormented. And Jesus saith unto him, I will come and heal him. The centurion answered and said, Lord, I am not worthy that thou shouldest come under my roof: but speak the word only, and my servant shall be healed. (Matthew 8:5–8)

Here is healing at a distance. That centurion understood divine authority, and the same divine authority is vested in the Christian, for Jesus is the pattern Christian.

For I am a man under authority, having soldiers under me: and I say to this man, Go, and he goeth; and to another, Come, and he cometh; and to my servant, Do this, and he doeth it. (Matthew 8:9)

The same divine authority that was vested in Jesus is vested by Jesus in every Christian soul. Jesus made provision for the church of Jesus Christ to go on forever and do the same things as He did and to keep on doing them forever. That is what is the matter with the church. The church has lost faith in that truth. The result, they went on believing He could save them from sin, but the other great range of Christian life was left to the doctors and the devil or anything else. And the church will never be a real church, in the real power of the living God again, until she comes back again to the original standard, where Jesus was.

Jesus said, "Behold, I give you authority." What authority? *"Against unclean spirits, to cast them out, and to heal all manner of sickness and all manner of disease"* (Matthew 10:1). Jesus has vested that authority in you. You say, "Well Lord, we understand the authority that is in Your Word, but we haven't the power." But Jesus said, *"Ye shall receive power, after that the Holy Ghost is come upon you"* (Acts 1:8).

Now the Holy Ghost is come upon every Christian in a measure. It is a question of degree! There are degrees of the measure of the Spirit of God in men's lives. The *baptism of the Holy Spirit* is a greater measure of the Spirit of God, but every man has a degree of the Holy Spirit in his life. You have. It is the Spirit in your life that gives you faith in God, that makes you a blessing to other people. It is the Holy Spirit that is *outbreathed* in your soul that touches another soul and moves them for God. Begin right where you are and let God take you along the Christian life as far as you like.

> *When Jesus heard it, he marveled, and said to them that followed. Verily I say unto you, I have not found so great faith, no, not in Israel.* (Matthew 8:10)

Jesus always commended faith when He met it. Jesus did not always meet faith. All the people who came to Jesus did not possess that order of faith. They had faith that if they got to Jesus, they would be healed. But here was a man who said, *"Speak the word only, and my servant shall be healed"* (verse 8).

Then you remember the case of the man at the pool of Bethesda. He did not even ask to be healed. As he lay there, Jesus walked up to him and said, *"Wilt thou be made whole?"* (John 5:6). He saw this poor chap who had been lying there for thirty-eight years, and Jesus did not wait for him to ask Him to heal. Jesus said, *"Wilt thou be made whole?"* and the poor fellow went on to say that when the water was troubled, he had no one to put him in, but while he was waiting another stepped in ahead of him. But Jesus said to him, *"Rise, take up thy bed, and walk"* (verse 8). He was made whole. Afterward, Jesus met him and said, *"Behold, thou art made whole: sin no more, lest a worse thing come unto thee"* (verse 14).

Most of sickness is the result of sin. That is the answer to the individual who sins. For thousands of years men have been sinning, and in consequence of their sin, they are diseased in their bodies. This will give you an idea. Scientists tell us there are tubercular germs in 90 percent of the population. The only difference is that when people keep in a healthy state, the germs do not get a chance to manifest themselves. I am trying to show the intimacy between sin and sickness, not necessarily the sin of the individual. It may never be the sin of the individual.

In records of the Lake and Graham family away back, tuberculosis was never known to them, until it appeared in my sister. My sister accompanied me to Africa, and she became so ill that when I got to Cape Town, we had to wait until her strength returned. God healed her.

Regarding people being healed at a distance, we receive telegrams from all over the world. Distance is no barrier to God. The United States has just finished the building of the greatest wireless station in the world. They send messages that register almost instantly across ten thousand miles. When the machine is touched here, it registers ten thousand miles away. Well, all right, when your *heart* strikes God in faith, it will register wherever that individual is, just that quick. All the discoveries of later years such as telegraph, telephone, wireless, and that sort of thing are just the common laws that Christians have practiced all their lives.

Nobody ever knelt down and prayed, but that the instant he touched God, his soul registered in Jesus Christ in glory, and the answer came back to the soul. Christians have that experience every day. The wise world has begun to observe that these laws are applicable in the natural realm. I asked Marconi once how he got his first idea for the wireless. He replied that he got it from watching an exhibition of telepathy in a cheap theater.

The prayer of the heart reaches God. Jesus replied to the leper, "I *will*; be clean." The next was the centurion's servant. The centurion said, "You do not need to come to my house. You *speak the word only*, and my servant shall be healed," and in His soul, Jesus said, "Be healed." Distance is no barrier to God. Distance makes no difference. The Spirit of God in you will go as far as your love reaches. *Love* is the medium that conveys the Spirit of God to another soul anywhere on God's earth.

This is what takes place as you pray. The Spirit of God comes upon you and bathes your soul, and a shaft of it reaches out and touches that soul over there. If you had an instrument that was fine enough to photograph spirit, you would discover this is done.

Is it not a marvelous thing that God has chosen us to be co-laborers with Him and that He takes us into partnership to do all that He is doing? Jesus Christ at the throne of God desires the blessing of you and me, and out of His holy heart the Spirit comes, and the soul is filled, and we cannot tell how or why.

I have known thousands of people to be healed who have never seen my face. They send a request for prayer, we pray, and we never hear anything more about them sometimes unless a friend or a neighbor or someone comes and tells us about them. Sometimes someone sends in a request for them. They will tell you they do not know what happened. They just got well. But you know why. That is the wonderful power there is in the Christian life, and that is the wonderful cooperation that the Lord Jesus has arranged between His own soul and the soul of the Christian. That is *the church, which is his body*" (Ephesians 1:22–23).

Jesus came to *"destroy the works of the devil"* (1 John 3:8). He healed all that were oppressed of the devil. (See Acts 10:38.) He did not use carnal weapons in destroying the work of the devil. He used a spiritual weapon. It is best expressed in Luke:

> And the whole multitude sought to touch him: for there went virtue [power] out of him, and healed them all.
>
> (Luke 6:19)

This is the perfect remedy for all of man's ills. Jesus taught His disciples the use of this weapon. He sent out the twelve, and He sent out the seventy. (See Luke 9:1–2, 10:1–19.) That His training was not fruitless is shown by the book of the Acts of the Apostles. Acting in the name of Jesus, the outflow of power from their lives brought healing to all who came to them. They duplicated His ministry. There is not one record of a failure in the book of Acts. The weapons of their warfare against the work of the devil in forms of sickness and disease were spiritual and not carnal. (See 2 Corinthians 10:4.) The same power is available today.

> Behold, I give unto you power to tread on serpents and scorpions, and over all the power of the enemy: and nothing shall by any means hurt you. (Luke 10:19)

God gives the members of the body of His Son power over the devil. He never gives the devil power over them.

One of the marvels of Christianity is the power given the believer. *"Resist the devil, and he will flee from you"* (James 4:7). The devil cannot make a believer do a single thing without the believer's consent or assent. Resist the devil and he flees. Give in and he wins. It is this fact, as simple as it may sound, that constitutes our responsibility for our behavior. So that no person can say, "I sinned in spite of myself," but he or she can only say, "I sinned because of myself."

Cleansed from all sin (root, stem, and branch) so that the devil has no anchor within and having put on the invincible armor of Ephesians 6, the believer is the master in every situation. If the believer stands firm and uses his armor efficiently, he is unbeatable by the devil.

Couple all that is said above with this statement from 1 John 4:4: *"Greater is he that is in you, than he that is in the world"*—why then should a believer ever give in to the devil and sin?

I can identify with Jesus as a member of His body when He said, *"The prince of this world cometh, and hath nothing in me"* (John 14:30). Why let the devil in or put anything in?

"And the God of peace shall bruise [shatter completely] *Satan under your feet shortly"* (Romans 16:20). In any warfare there comes a time when the enemy is shattered. Stand true and allow God to shatter him under your feet. Stand fast!

Chapter 12

Are the Days of Miracles Past?

∿✦∿

Pamphlet

Among the shrewdest and most damaging lies that was ever told was Satan's lie that the days of miracles are past. And the shrewdness of it is in the fact that he got the church, her priests, ministers, and preachers to tell the lie. It has produced more infidels, created more unbelief concerning God than perhaps any other lie. But the days of miracles are never past and never will be past so long as Jesus Christ remains "the same yesterday, today, and forever." (See Hebrews 13:8; 1 Corinthians 12:8–12; Matthew 8:1–17; Mark 16:17.) Read the following testimonies.

Healing of G. Y. Locke, M.D., Portland, Oregon, August 6, 1921

It gives me the greatest pleasure of my life to testify that I, Dr. Genevieve Y. Locke, Office: 708 Dekum Building, Residence: 535 Yamhill, Phone: Auto 527–72, received instant healing from the mighty prayer of Dr. Lake.

About three weeks ago last Wednesday, I suffered a broken rib, causing great agony, the shock affecting my heart. I was positive at the time that I had a broken a rib and went soon afterwards to the office of one of the leading chiropractic doctors of the city, had him examine me on the operating table, and to my great surprise, he told me there was nothing wrong, there were no broken ribs. So, trying to hold up under great suffering in the strength of his theory, I continued to work in my home under difficulties until one Saturday, I was unable to arise from bed at all. I was simply exhausted from trying to hold up under the strain all of this time, as no doubt everyone knows the seriousness of a broken bone without proper attention.

I knew that my condition was very serious, even critical, yet tried to hide the truth from my friends and loved ones. I was growing weaker and weaker, facing an operation from the medical point of view, believing it to be the only chance. I had the very best physician in Portland called to my bedside. I say the best, because he did not try to hide the seriousness of my case from me; but to my surprise, he looked into my eyes and told me the truth with all the heartfelt sympathy that any man or woman can give another. I thanked and blessed him as he left my bedside.

He made a second call, only to say the same as before and to add that I was growing weaker each hour, that my entire body had become affected by the poisonous fluid that had accumulated around the broken rib, and that my heart was leaking until one could hardly feel the circulation.

Two specialists were called to my bedside, only to verify the statements of the first physician. By this time, however, my loved ones and friends had began to realize the seriousness of my condition and were suffering with me, the pain being too great to be suffered silently. My business affairs are always kept in shape so that in case of death, there would be nothing to disturb those left behind. I gave myself up into the silence that no one feels until death is hovering near and said, "Blessed Savior, not my will, but Thine be done."

All was well with me as I have always tried to live close to God. Just at that minute, at three o'clock in the afternoon, a voice out of somewhere whispered the name Dr. John G. Lake. Instantly, I had him called. As soon as he received the message, he came immediately to my home. It was four o'clock when he arrived, and I was gasping for breath with the chill of death all over my body. He came to my bedside with his kind, gentle smile that I have since found so characteristic of him, and with the divine love of God that is within him, and knelt at my bedside to pray.

The look of faith in his eyes that reflected to me his own soul gave me the confidence and assurance that even death could be overcome by being close to God in prayer. He spoke only a word or two to me. The bandage around my body, which was to support the broken rib, seemed to be a hundred pound weight that was crushing me. As he prayed with faith, it seemed as though that bandage was slipping, for I began to breathe without the slightest effort and realized the wondrous and marvelous fact that I was receiving instant healing. I could not keep from crying out, "Oh blessed Savior, I am breathing in the breath of life." Dr. Lake knew what had taken place; he smiled and said, "You are well and can get out of bed whenever you want to," but advised me to keep a little quiet for a few days.

He left as quietly as he had come, just as though he had not just proven to myself and friends that he could heal today just as Jesus did. Who could possibly question his relationship to God after such a demonstration of the love of God and the lifting up a soul from the very throes of death?

After he had left the house, I sat up in bed to show my friends that I was no longer sick, that God had healed me as sure as there is a God in heaven. I talked and sang, and next morning could scarcely wait to get to the phone to tell Dr. Lake the good news of my perfect healing. I feel so happy and free that I would just love to take the whole world in my arms and tell them the glad tidings that God does and will heal, and it is the only thing that can and will last, God's divine love.

Baby Barnes Healed from Death

One of the touching healings is that of the little babe of Mrs. May Barnes of Washougal, Washington. She wrote a pitiful letter of entreaty to us for prayer for her baby, who was born a "blue baby." She said, "Oh, Dr. Lake, do not let my baby die! Do not let my baby die! Oh, Dr. Lake, you are a father yourself; do not let my baby die." And again, "Oh, Dr. Lake, pray. Pray. Do not let my baby die."

The child had suffered from a weak heart and malnutrition from birth and had three dreadful ruptures, one in each groin and a great naval rupture. She was advised to bring the baby to Dr. Lake. The child was so withered away that it looked like a little wizened up alligator. The power of God came upon the child as prayer was offered, and it began to mend and eat and sleep as other babes. It took on flesh and grew plump and rosy, and when she returned to her home, the babe was perfectly well with the exception of one rupture. So one day soon after, she returned with the babe; the rupture was inflamed and painful; but as hands were laid upon the child in prayer, the rupture was instantly healed; and though the child has since had a severe attack of whooping cough, there has been no return of the rupture or other sickness.

More Testimonies

Mr. George Alley was stricken with pneumonia and reported dying. Two of our ministers went to him. When prayer was offered, he was so blessed and healed that he soon fell asleep. Not knowing that the man had already received healing, Dr. Wallace and his wife went to the house and found that the family was asleep; so they did not trouble to awaken the people, but knelt down in the dark on the front porch and prayed. When they had ceased to pray, Dr. Wallace told his wife that he had heard from God and that the man was well, and he was.

On Friday night last, fifty-two testimonies of recent miracles of healing were given. These testimonies included healings through absent prayer in Norway, Great Britain, Africa, and Canada, besides many who were healed at the healing rooms.

Since out last circular was issued, we have had two great public meetings, one at the auditorium. The *Oregonian* reported an attendance of more than three thousand persons; 363 persons testified by rising, to being healed by the power of God. Also, special testimonies were presented, which were: Dr. Wood, instantly healed of paralytic stroke as Dr. Lake laid hands on her in prayer; Mrs. Mary Matheny, healed of forty cancers; F. J. Kelly, healed of multiple sclerosis; Grover Risdon, healed of malformed head and was dumb and paralyzed, believed to be the greatest miracle of healing in the world; Mrs. Ione Stanton, healed from death of glandular tuberculosis; Mr. Roy Ferguson, whose testimony appears in this pamphlet, was healed out of a plaster cast; and many others.

Another great public meeting was held at Oaks Park Rink. A New York medical specialist who was present pronounced it the most remarkable religious meeting he had ever attended, if not the most wonderful ever held in the world. He pronounced Dr. Lake's address given on this occasion of surpassing power and convincing force and the miracles of healing genuine beyond all question. He visited Dr. Locke and personally examined her and pronounced her absolutely healed.

Affidavit

Head Bookkeeper for the Industrial Insurance Commission Healed of Tuberculosis of the Spine

I, Roy Ferguson, herewith certify, praise God, I am well and perfectly healed and realize the solemnity of this oath. I was twenty-nine years of age the seventh of last January, a resident of Salem, Oregon, 775 S. 13th Street. While head bookkeeper for the Industrial Insurance Commission, I was stricken with a severe sickness, diagnosed as tuberculosis of the bone. The doctors amputated my left leg close to the thigh to try to check the spread of the disease throughout my entire body.

It was a useless effort. The disease next appeared in my spine, until four vertebrae were affected and in a process of dissolution. I was then placed in a plaster of Paris cast, and my suffering was terrible. I came to Dr. Lake's Divine Healing Institute, 129 4th Street, Portland, Oregon, and in answer to prayer was instantly healed. My years of agony are over. I am now perfectly well, have put on flesh rapidly, and am praising God continually for His saving and healing power, and am praying God's blessing upon Dr. Lake and his people continuously.

Signed,
—Roy Ferguson

The healing rooms are open at 10 AM to 10 PM for personal and private ministry through prayer and the laying on of hands. Divine Healing Teaching Meetings every day of the week at 3 PM. At the close of this service, all who desire are ministered to for any need of body, soul, or spirit. If you are a doubter, come and see, and tell us what it is worth to you. If you are an unbeliever, bring your sick friends or come with your own difficulty, be blessed of God, and test what it is worth to you. If you are a professed Christian with little faith in God, come and be vitalized by the Spirit and tell us what it is worth to you. If you are the ordinary man or woman of the world and have paid no attention to religious things and have a question mark in your mind, come and see for yourself and decide how much it is worth to you and if real Christianity that gets results and demonstrates them is worth the price.

Chapter 13

Pneumatology

Sermon

*The blind receive their sight, and the lame walk, the
lepers are cleansed, and the deaf hear, the dead are raised
up, and the poor have the gospel preached to them.*
—Matthew 11:5

Somebody has lied. Who is it? The preachers of many of the regular churches, theologians, professors in almost every university and college, and the man who has not investigated have all said that the days of miracles are past. We contend that the days of miracles are here now, they always have been here, and always will be here to him who hath faith in God. We contend that God answers prayer today as readily as God ever did; and further, that the same faith that has received an answer once will bring an answer from God again; that the same power of the Spirit of God that moved upon the waters and that performed wonders both in nature and in man, both in the spiritual and the physical, is still available. It is here in Portland. It is at work every

173

day. If you do not believe it, come to our healing rooms and observe for yourself.

The Blind Receive Their Sight

Mr. Adam Streit of St. Johns, Portland, was blind for several years in both eyes. He was ministered to on three different occasions through prayer and the laying on of hands by the ministry of The Church at Portland. He is now perfectly healed and gave public testimony to his healing in The Church at Portland, at 129 4th Street, a few days ago.

The Lame Walk

A most conspicuous case, Mr. Roy Ferguson, head bookkeeper for the State Industrial Insurance Commission at Salem, the state capital, was stricken with tuberculosis of the bone. The disease affecting the spine, he was encased in a plaster of Paris cast and confined to his bed for more than a year. One leg was amputated just below the hip in the hope of checking the progress of the disease, but without avail.

He was abandoned to die by his physicians and brought to Portland specialists who said nothing could be done. He was brought to the healing rooms, was prayed for, and God instantly healed him. He is well. He was saved from his sins and baptized in the Holy Ghost and is now ministering this power of God to others and is one of the representatives of our work in Salem, Oregon.

The Deaf Hear

Mrs. Mary Evans of Corvallis, Oregon, was deaf for twenty years. She heard of the healing of Mr. Roy Ferguson through friends and came to Portland to visit the healing rooms. She called Dr. Lake on the phone to come to the Multnomah Hotel parlors where, in the presence of a group of friends and others from the city who were present, she was ministered to and was instantly healed and conversed freely with her friends and Dr. Lake. She reported by long distance phone today that her healing was perfect and she will come to Portland in the near future to give public testimony and praise to God in The Church at Portland.

I, Harley Day, 189 Mill Street, Portland, 18 years and nine months old, being first duly sworn and realizing fully the solemnity of this my oath, do testify: I was born dumb and was thereby unable to speak, also my nasal passages were malformed so that it was impossible for me to breathe through my nose. I under went six surgical operations on my throat, but was not benefited and gave up in despair.

Lately, friends advised me to go to Dr. John G. Lake, divine healer, which I did. Dr. Lake prayed for me at the close of the evening service, laying his hands on my throat. As he prayed, a stream of healing power poured from his hands and diffused itself through my entire person. Instantly something in my throat relaxed and a sense of freedom came upon me. In his prayer Dr. Lake prayed that the dumb demon be cast out. I felt at once that it was done, and in a few minutes I began to speak, and each day I am able to speak with greater clearness.

On another occasion, as prayer was offered and hands laid upon me in faith, my nasal passages opened, and I have been able to breathe through my nose naturally ever since. I have become a sincere Christian and am now a member of Dr. Lake's church and praise my Lord for His saving grace and healing power.

Signed,
—Harley Day

Lepers Are Cleansed

Mrs. I___ S____ of Council Crest, Portland, a beautiful, cultured, high-class woman, became diseased so that a score of physicians and institutions assured her there was no possibility of recovery through medical assistance. The disease progressed until she was a skeleton, her throat became so badly affected from the disease that her power of speech was almost entirely ruined, and her mind became affected. She was brought to the healing rooms, ministered to, and as prayer was offered and hands laid upon her, the power of God came mightily upon her and the disease was destroyed.

There began from that moment a gradual reconstruction of her entire person. She is now in perfect health and soundness of mind, the bloom of wholesome, healthy womanhood in her face, the joy of God in her soul, the peace of God in her heart, and the victory of God in her life. She was baptized in the Holy Spirit and has begun, in turn, to minister the same blessed Spirit to other lives.

The Dead Are Raised Up

Mrs. W. E. Stoughton, Portland, Oregon, was sick of double pneumonia, hemorrhaging over a pint of blood at one time. We knelt by her bedside while she was in the very throes of death; and even as we prayed, her heart ceased to beat, her respiration stopped, and she lapsed into apparent death. We continued to pray; nine long minutes passed before evidence of returning life was manifest. We continued in faith and prayer, but in less than twenty minutes another lapse came, this time eleven-and-a-half minutes of seeming death, and yet again thirteen minutes, and then came the final struggle when for nineteen minutes no evidence of life was apparent.

We believe that the spirit and body were kept united through the persistent and unwavering faith of those who prayed. At two-thirty in the morning, the glory of God burst from her soul and flooded her with the joy and the presence of God. She was perfectly healed and arose from her bed glorifying God—a well woman.

Her little daughter, Beaulah, was healed of cancer of the mouth after surgeons had said the child's life could only be saved through an operation to remove a portion of the roof of the mouth, which would have destroyed her speech. She was healed through faith in Jesus Christ; not only the cancer disappeared, but she was also healed of leakage of the heart through prayer at The Church at Portland.

The Poor Have the Gospel Preached to Them

Day by day, we go among the poor and the lame and the halt and the blind, sin-stricken and disease-smitten, ministering God's blessed love and power, fulfilling once more the declaration of Jesus, the mark and stamp of real Christianity, "The poor have the gospel preached to them."

These Signs Shall Follow Them That Believe

> These signs shall follow them that believe; In my name
> shall they cast out devils; they shall speak with new
> tongues; they shall take up serpents; and if they drink
> any deadly thing, it shall not hurt them; they shall lay
> hands on the sick, and they shall recover.
>
> (Mark 16:17–18)

Chapter 14

Is It Worth the Price?

❧❦❧

Pamphlet

Our fellow citizen, O. G. Blake of Number 10, 9th Street, Portland, Oregon, was abandoned to die by his physicians of diabetic gangrene. The entire foot and lower limb were in a state of mortification. The stench of the rotting foot would almost drive one from the room. With tears, his physicians bade him goodbye and left him to die. *Materia Medica*[7] had no remedy. The medical expert said, "I am stumped; there is nothing I can do for you further." Amputations were useless, as the diabetic state permeated his whole person.

He called Reverend John G. Lake of The Church at Portland, a businessman's church in the Gordon Building, 283 Stark Street, conducted by preachers who are businessmen. One of the ministering staff was sent to minister to this

---

[7] *Materia Medica:* a treatise on the substances used in the composition of medical remedies; a branch of medical science that deals with the sources, nature, properties, and preparation of drugs. *Merriam-Webster's 11th Collegiate Dictionary* CD-ROM, © 2003.

dying man. He is perfectly healed. What science could not do, God accomplished.

His big toe rotted off. He has it in a bottle of alcohol. You can see it. New flesh and bone grew on. He is walking around the city and has taken his place again as one of the heads of the Yeoman Society of the state of Oregon.

Fellow citizens, what is it worth to you? What is it worth to his home? What is it worth to his wife? What is it worth to Portland? What is it worth to Oregon? What is it worth to the United States? What is it worth to the world? What is it worth to the kingdom of heaven?

Affidavits

I, Mrs. D. C. Tappan of 874 Pardee Street, Portland, Oregon, being first duly sworn under oath, depose and say that I am 63 years of age, of a sound mind, and that I make the following statement fully realizing the sacredness of my oath: That two years ago a cancer formed on the end of my spine, and it grew and spread in the form of a horseshoe until it became three inches in diameter, causing me great pain constantly. Many physicians of Portland and Seattle treated me from time to time, but the cancer steadily grew worse and discharged more and more.

When all our funds were exhausted in this way, and complete hopelessness and despair settled down over my family, and I was facing a miserable death, a friend sent word to us that Dr. Lake was praying for the sick and was having wonderful cures through prayer. A new hope was born in our hearts, and we immediately sought him that his associates—Dr. Lake being absent from the city—would pray for us. His secretary, Reverend Harriet Graham, knelt with me and most earnestly prayed God to deliver me from this cancer. Immediately, all the terrible pain left my body and has never returned.

During the intervening three months, the cancer continued to dry up, and now there is nothing left but the scar to remind me of those awful days. No one can ever know how the sun shines on us after the hand of God has touched the body and scattered all our clouds.

My daughter was also a great sufferer from violent headaches. It was she who brought me to the healers, and without especially being prayed for, when the healing came to me, she was also touched by its power, and she, too, was immediately healed.

Signed,

Mrs. D. C. Tappan

Subscribed and sworn to before me, a Notary Public for the State of Oregon, this 11th day of October, 1920. My commission expires Jan. 29, 1924.   D. N. McInturff, Notary Public

Witnesses:

H. H. Marble.

Mrs. Margaret Higgins

❧◦◦✦◦◦❧

What is it worth to you to know that God answers prayer today? How much is it worth to you to know that even after the best physicians in the land have despaired, that God will heal all who come to Him? How much is it worth to you to know that when the church tells you that the days of miracles are past, that they lie?

◦◦◦◦◦◦

We, Mr. and Mrs. Marble of 1004 E. 32nd Street, being first duly sworn under oath, depose and say that we both are of mature age and of sound mind and make the following statement fully realizing the sacredness of such an oath: Our daughter, Edith May Marble, seventeen years of age, contracted flu eight months ago, which caused pleurisy and developed into tuberculosis. She went down to death, and by September fifteenth she was in the very throes of death. We had six doctors, but she steadily grew worse. She was operated on and seemed some better for a few days, but again sank rapidly.

Mr. Wright, of Reverend Lake's healing rooms, was called and prayer offered. A week later, she vomited quantities of digitalis, which had accumulated in her system during her sickness, which was given her in course of treatment. She began to recover, and the wound healed. She is now up and walking around, praising God, eating well, taking on flesh rapidly. We desire the public to know of this miracle of God's power and give thanks for these godly people who brought the light of divine healing to us.

Signed,

Mr. and Mrs. H. H. Marble

Subscribed and sworn to before me, a Notary Public for the State of Oregon, this 11th day of

October, 1920. My Commission expires Jan. 29, 1924. D. N. McInturff, Notary Public

⊸❦⊱

What is it worth to you to know that God is healing tuberculosis? What is it worth to you to know that God will save your dear ones from the grave? What is it worth to you to know that all sickness, sin, and disease do not come from God, but that they belong to the evil one?

⊸❦⊱

Mr. Frank Roles of the Pacific Agency, Inc., in the Swetland Building, one of the leading real estate brokers of the Pacific Coast, was stricken with a violent attack of neuritis until his cries of agony resounded through the house. He says: "My suffering was so intense that I could not keep from crying out."

Mr. E. S. Anderson of Royal Court, an ordained deacon of The Church at Portland, of which John G. Lake is overseer, with his wife, was called to his bedside. Moved by his terrible suffering, they fell upon their knees and laid their hands upon him. The power of God came upon him. He was instantly healed and in fifteen minutes was out of pain. He slept like a child and next day returned to his office.

⊸❦⊱

Citizen, what is this fact worth to you? What is it worth to know that God is not far away? What is it worth to you to know that "*Jesus Christ* [is] *the same yesterday, and to day, and for ever*"? (Hebrews 13:8).

⊸❦⊱

Harold Rooney, grandson of Mrs. Josephine Raymond of 2914 Fairmont Street, Vancouver, Washington, seven years old, was an epileptic, subject to fits from infancy. He became dumb. His mind became affected. The physicians said, "There is not a thing can be done for him." He was brought to Reverend Lake's healing rooms, 283 Stark Street Prayer was offered. The epileptic demon was cast out. The fits ceased. His speech returned. His mind became normal, and he put on flesh rapidly and is now a rosy, healthy, happy boy, attending school.

∼⊶≺∭≻⊷∼

Fellow citizen, what is this cute by the power of God worth to you? It has saved the expense of an inmate for life in a state institution. It has restored to society a life that will add wealth to the nation, citizenship to the state, a home and family to the city of Portland—a man with faith in God, and a Christian to the kingdom of heaven.

∼⊶≺∭≻⊷∼

Dr. D. N. McInturff, a man with a successful law practice, a Supreme Court lawyer of note, seeing these things, gave up his practice of law and became pastor of The Church at Portland. He himself ministers to the sick, and they are healed. Last week among the numerous healings under his ministry, there were three cases of blindness. What is it worth to hear the shout of joy when blind eyes open by the power of God sufficient to heal blindness?

Reverend Harriett Graham, a professional nurse, hospital matron, herself a miracle of healing by the Lord, is also one of Dr. Lake's associates, and under her wonderful ministry people are healed every day.

Dr. Herman Wallace, noted divine businessman, author, and economist, is on our staff. He is a thinker of thinkers and a man of exceptional spiritual power. Realizing the wonderful possibilities of Dr. Lake's undertaking for Portland and the world, he has become one of the ministering staff.

Reverend William O. Wright operated a stock ranch in the state of Wyoming. He was discharged from the United States Army at the close of the war and was pronounced incurable. More than a hundred X-ray pictures were taken of his person by the government experts in their effort to determine the nature of the disease. He was operated upon many times without success. His case is a matter of government record.

He says, "When suffering the agonies of the damned, I was ministered to by Reverend Lake, Reverend Harriet Graham, and others. The Lord healed me. He filled me with His Spirit, and I now minister to the sick throughout the city who are confined to their homes and are unable to be brought to the healing rooms."

Mr. Blake, whose healing appears at the head of this pamphlet, was one of his patients. He will call at your home anywhere if you so desire.

❦

What is this life worth to the United States? What is it worth to Portland? What is it worth to see hundreds of healed and saved people gather together in The Church at Portland, giving thanks to God? What is it worth to Portland to foster and sustain this work and thereby become the healthiest city on earth?

Chapter 15

Lake and Divine Healing Investigated

~~~❖~~~

Pamphlet · By Dr. John G. Lake

Divine Healing Institute
615 Broadway, · San Diego, California
Meetings Daily 2:30 and 7:30 · Price: 25 cents

How God Healed in Spokane, Washington

On June 15 we were waiting at our healing rooms by a committee of the Better Business Bureau of the city of Spokane, whose duty in part it is to investigate the truthfulness of all public announcements appearing in the city papers. For some time previous to this, we had been publishing some of the wonderful testimonies of healing by the power of God that had taken place in the daily course of our ministry at the Divine Healing Institute.

Among the testimonies that had appeared was the wonderful testimony of Mrs. John A. Graham, née[8] Peterson,

---

[8] *née*: born, used to identify a married woman by her maiden family name. *Merriam-Webster's 11th Collegiate Dictionary* CD-ROM, © 2003.

whose healing astonished the medical world. The testimony of Reverend Joseph Osborne, left to die of Bright's disease at the Deaconess hospital, analysis showing 15 percent albumen; Reverend Charles B. LeDoux, healed when in very death from pneumonia; Mrs. Mary Mere, Mrs. Leana Lakey, Grover Risdon, baby Agnes Young, Mrs. Mary Matheny, of Portland, Oregon, who was healed of forty cancers, and others.

These testimonies were so astounding that complaints reached the Better Business Bureau to the effect that the testimonies must certainly be untrue. The Better Business Bureau promptly undertook an investigation, and the call at our healing rooms was for that purpose.

In the presence of the committee, as they waited, we called eighteen persons whose testimonies had appeared in the public print, who in turn gave testimony as to their own condition and the wonder of their healing by the power of God in the name of the Lord Jesus Christ under this ministry. After eighteen had been examined, we presented them with names of many healed persons in the city, desiring them to go personally to these persons and investigate for themselves whether these things were so.

Realizing the amount of labor necessary for a proper investigation, I suggested to the committee that on Sunday, June 23, at three o'clock in the afternoon at our public service, we would present one hundred cases of healed persons for their investigation and invited them to form a committee composed of physicians, lawyers, judges, educators, and businessmen, who should tender a verdict.

In the days lapsing between the interview at the healing rooms and Sunday, June 23, the committee continued their investigation, interviewing persons whose names we had furnished them. On Friday, June 21, before out great Sunday meeting, we received a letter from the committee, assuring us that they had no desire in any way to interfere with the good that we were doing and gently let themselves down so that their appearance at the Sunday meeting would not be necessary. Two members of the committee saw us privately and said that the committee was astounded. They said, "We soon found out, upon investigation, you did not tell half of it."

One of the committee was visiting at Davenport, Washington, where the firm had a branch store. As he looked around the store, he found printed announcements advertising a meeting which we were about to conduct at Davenport. He made inquiry from the manager as to these announcements were being made through their store, and the manager replied as follows:

> The whole countryside around Davenport is aflame with surprise at the marvelous healing of a girl in this community, well-known to me, and, I believe, well-known to yourself, Miss Louise Reinboldt, daughter of Mr. Jake Reinboldt.
>
> About three-and-a-half years ago, Miss Reinboldt and her sister were operated on for what the doctors thought was appendicitis. The one girl died as the result of the operation. Louise came out of it unable to speak. She was taken to throat specialists, who pronounced her case absolutely incurable. Recently she was taken to Spokane to Mr. Lake's healing rooms and ministered to for twenty-six days. On the twenty-sixth day, she startled her mother and family and, in fact, the whole countryside, by calling her mother on the long distance telephone and announcing to her in plain words the fact that she was healed.

While preparing for her daily visit to the healing rooms, she suddenly discovered herself whistling, and said to herself, "If I can whistle, I can speak also," and so discovered the paralyzed condition of her throat was truly healed.

Other members of the committee reported similar remarkable healings, and not being desirous of becoming a public laughingstock, they hastily wrote as above quoted.

Mr. Lake, however, announced that there would be no change in the program, but that the meeting as announced would take place, and if the Better Business Bureau would not take their place, he would appeal to the public for a verdict. The meeting took place at the Masonic Temple before a large audience estimated by the police to number thousands, hundreds being compelled to stand throughout the entire service, and hundreds were refused admittance.

After a brief statement by Dr. Lake on the reasons for the meeting and of the desire to glorify God by permitting the city and the world to know that Jesus Christ has never changed, that prayer was answerable today as it ever was, and that the days of miracles had not passed, but were forever possible through the exercise of faith in God, the following testimonies were given:

Reverend R. Armstrong, a Methodist minister, of N2819 Columbus Avenue, who had a sarcoma growing out of the left shoulder three times as large as a man's head, was healed in answer to prayer.

Reverend Thomas B. O'Reilly, of 430 Rookery Building, testified to being healed of fits so violent that when stricken with them it required seven policemen to overpower and confine him in the hospital, and of his instantaneous healing and perfect restoration to health through the prayer of faith.

Baby Agnes Young, N169 Post Street, healed of extreme malnutrition. A patient at the Deaconess hospital for nine months, from the time of birth until her healing, she weighed six-and-a-half pounds at birth and at the age of nine months, only four-and-a-half pounds. One evening, when one of the ministers from Reverend Lake's healing rooms called to minister to her, she was found in the dead room. The nurse, believing her to be dead, had removed her to the dead room. He took the child in his arms, praying the prayer of faith; God heard and answered. He removed her from the hospital and placed her in the hands of a Christian woman for nursing. In six weeks, she was perfectly well and strong. The father and mother arose to corroborate the testimony. They are both members of Dr. Lake's church.

Mrs. Chittenden, pastor of the Church of the Truth at Coeur d'Alene, Idaho, testified to her healing of cancers of the breast; one breast having been removed in an operation and the other breast becoming likewise affected with cancer. She was healed of the Lord in answer to prayer.

Mrs. Everetts, 1911 Boone Avenue, testified to her healing of varicose veins. She had suffered from them for thirty-eight years. The veins were enlarged until they were the size of goose eggs in spots. Under the right knee there was a sack of blood so large that the knee was made stiff. She had exhausted every medical method. After being ministered to at the healing rooms for a short period, she was entirely well and the veins are perfectly clear.

Mrs. Constance Hoag, Puyallup, Washington, broke her kneecap. A section of the bone protruded through the flesh.

She wrote requesting that the ministers of the healing rooms lay their hands upon a handkerchief in faith and prayer and send it to her in accordance with Acts 19:12. This was done. She applied the handkerchief to the knee and in fifteen minutes the pain had gone, and in an hour the bone had returned to place and was perfectly healed.

Mrs. Walker, Granby Court, was an invalid at the Deaconess hospital from internal cancer; after an exploratory operation she was pronounced incurable by the doctors. She also had a severe case of neuritis. Her suffering was unspeakable. She testified to her healing and of her restoration to perfect health, the cancer having passed from her body in seven sections. Since then, many have been healed through her prayer and faith.

Mrs. John A. Graham, E369 Hartson, a nurse and hospital matron, was operated on for fibroid tumors. The generative organs were removed, and at a later date, she was operated on a second time for gallstones. The operation not being a success, she was eventually left to die; and when in the throes of death and unconscious, she was healed by the power of God in answer to prayer of one of the ministers called from the healing rooms. The organs that had been removed in the operation regrew in the body, and she became a normal woman and a mother.

Mr. Asa Hill, a farmer from Palouse, Washington, testified that he had been a rheumatic cripple for fifteen years and was instantly healed at a meeting conducted by Mr. Lake, through prayer with the laying on of hands. The meeting was held at a theater in Moscow, Idaho.

Mrs. Wolverton was injured in a Great Northern railroad wreck and was awarded large damages by the court. (See court record.) Physicians testified her injuries to be such that motherhood was impossible. After her marriage, the physician's testimony was confirmed. She was healed in answer to prayer and gave birth to a son and since has given birth to twins.

Miss Jennie Walsh, S116 Fiske Street, had a disease of the gall bladder, which became filled with pus. Her physicians insisted on an immediate operation to save her life. Mr. Lake laid hands upon her in prayer at eleven o'clock PM. Ten minutes afterward her pain ceased, the pus emptied from the bladder naturally, and she was entirely healed.

Mrs. Lamphear, 115½ Sprague Avenue, was an invalid for eleven years, suffering from prolapse of the stomach, bowels, and uterus, and also from tuberculosis and rheumatism. Her husband carried her from place to place in his arms. After eleven years of terrible suffering, upon the advice of her physicians, who were unable to assist her, she was sent to Soap Lake, Oregon, for bath treatments. Ordinary baths had no effect on her, and the superintendent testified that they had finally placed her in super-heated baths, hotter than they had ever put any human being in before.

Through this treatment, an abnormal growth was started in the left leg and foot. Her leg became three inches longer than the other, and her foot one inch too long. A bone as large as an orange grew on the knee. She received an instant healing of rheumatism. The leg shortened at the rate of an inch a week, the foot also shortened to its normal length, and the bone growth on the knee totally disappeared. Her tuberculosis was healed, and she is praising God for His goodness. She was born without the outer lobe of one ear; it also grew on.

Mrs. Ben Eastman, née Koch, 1115 First Avenue, was pronounced incurable from tubercular glands by 73 physicians. She was operated on 26 times and remained in the same dying condition. Later she was taken to the Osteopathic Institute in Los Angeles, California, and was a patient there for three-and-a-half years. Her father testified that his daughter's illness cost him three houses in the city of Davenport, a valuable wheat ranch of 160 acres, 147 carloads of wood, and all the money he had. She is now healed of the Lord, and since then has become the happy wife of Mr. Ben Eastman.

Mrs. Carter, of S714 Sherman Street, wife of Policeman Carter, was examined by seven physicians who pronounced her to be suffering from a fibroid tumor, estimated to weigh fifteen pounds. She was ministered to at the healing rooms at four-thirty in the afternoon and at eleven o'clock the next day, returned to the healing rooms perfectly healed and wearing her corsets. The enormous tumor dematerialized. (See her wonderful testimony in our pamphlet, "The Story of S714 Sherman Street.")

Mrs. O. D. Stutsman, Hansen Apartments, testified to having been an invalid for thirteen years. On one occasion, she lay in the Sacred Heart Hospital with a twenty-pound weight attached to her foot for thirty-two days, while suffering from inflammatory rheumatism. Her suffering was so intense that she begged her husband to take her home, preferring to remain a cripple rather than endure such suffering. The Reverend Lake was called to minister to her at her home; as prayer was offered, the power of the Spirit of God surged through her. Five minutes after his hands were laid upon her, she arose from her bed, perfectly healed.

Mr. John Dewitt, of Granby Court, testified on behalf of Frederick Barnard, thirty-two years of age, who was injured in his babyhood from a fall from a baby cab, causing curvature of the spine. As he grew to boyhood and manhood he was never able to take part in the sports common to boyhood and manhood. When the great war came on, he would stand around the recruiting office, longing and covetously watching the men who enlisted for the war. One day he expressed to Mr. Dewitt the sorrow of his soul that he was not able to enlist also. Mr. Dewitt told him of Mr. Lake's healing rooms and invited him to come and be ministered to. The curvature of his spine straightened, and his height increased one inch. He applied for enlistment in the Canadian army and was accepted by the army physician as first class and sent abroad.

God in Surgery

Mrs. O. Gilbertson, N4115 Helena Street, testified that through disease her hip came out of joint and her limb would turn like the leg of a doll, showing that it was entirely out of the socket. Her home is about five miles distant from the healing rooms. Reverend Lake and his co-workers engaged in prayer for her at the healing rooms; and as prayer was offered the power of God came upon her, resetting the joint.

◦◦◦◦◦

The following remarks were made by the Reverend Lake as the testimony was given: "Do you hear it, you folks who worship a dead Christ? You doctors hear it? You preachers who lie to the people and say the days of miracles are past, do you hear it? You doubters hear it? God set the woman's hip. Because faith in God applied the blessed power of God to her life and limb."

❧❀⟨❈⟩❀☙

Now comes one of the most remarkable cases in history. The Risdon family stood holding their six-year-old son on their shoulders. This boy was born with a closed head. In consequence, as he increased in years, the skull was forced upward like the roof of a house, the forehead and the back of the head also being forced out in similar manner, giving the head the appearance of the hull of a yacht upside down. The pressure on the brain caused the right side to become paralyzed, and the child was dumb.

Physicians said that nothing could be done for him until he was twelve years old, and then the entire top of the head would have to be removed, the sides of the skull expanded and the entire head covered with a silver plate. Under divine healing ministration, in answer to prayer, the bones softened, the head expanded, the skull was reduced to its normal size, the paralysis disappeared, and the dumbness was gone. He speaks like other children and now attends the public school.

❧❀⟨❈⟩❀☙

Remarks by Reverend Lake: "I want you to see that in the Spirit of God there is a science far beyond physical or psychological science and the man or woman who enters into the Spirit relation with God and exercises. His power is most scientific; that the power of God in this instance was sufficient to soften the bones of the head, expand the skull, and bring the head down to normal when the child was four-and-a-half years old—something that no medicine could do and no surgical operation could accomplish without endangering the life of the child."

Casting Out of Demons and Healing of the Insane

Mrs. Lena Lakey, W116 Riverside Avenue, testified of having suffered with violent insanity. She was a cook at a lumber camp. She told of the men at the camp endeavoring to overpower her and tie her in the bed; of her tearing the bed to pieces and breaking her arms free; of how she struck one man with the side of the bed, rendering him unconscious. Another was in the hospital three weeks, recovering from injuries. She escaped into the woods in a drenching rain, eventually falling exhausted in a copse of trees, where she lay unconscious for six hours until a searching party found her.

She was brought to Spokane in an auto by six men and was tied with ropes. Before taking her to the court to be committed to the insane asylum, they decided to take her to the healing rooms. Reverend Lake laid his hands on her in prayer, and the demons were cast out and she was instantly healed. An abscess in her side, from which she had suffered for fifteen years, totally disappeared in twenty-four hours, and a rheumatic bone deposit between the joints of the fingers and toes, so extensive that it forced the joint apart, was gone in forty-eight hours. She was made *every whit whole* (John 7:23).

Mrs. Holder gave testimony of healing by the power of God in answer to prayer, having been healed from insanity while an inmate of the Medical Lake Insane Asylum, in answer to the prayers of Mr. Lake and his assistants.

Other Incurables

Mr. and Mrs. Harry Lotz stood, holding their baby in their arms. The baby developed pus in the kidney and was pronounced incurable by several physicians. The child was brought to the healing rooms. Reverend Lake laid his hands upon the child in prayer, and it was instantly healed.

Mr. Allen, pastor of the Pentecostal mission, was dying of pellagra. He was carried unconscious from the train. The men thought him to be dead and put him in the baggage room. He was instantly healed through the laying on of hands and prayer. His case is a matter of record by the government pellagra investigation commission.

Mrs. Ben Long, 1971 Atlantic Street, testified to being instantly healed of paralysis of the left side. She was brought to the healing rooms and ministered to by Dr. Lake, and when ten feet from the healing room door, she found that she had been made whole. Discovering that she was well, she returned to the waiting room and showed herself to Mr. Lake and offered praise to God for her healing.

Mrs. John Dewitt, Granby Court, gave testimony to having been healed of neuritis after years of suffering. Later she was healed when in a state of apparent death following two strokes. A group of friends were present and witnessed her instant healing as Reverend Lake prayed.

Mrs. Mary Mero, lady-in-waiting at the healing rooms, who resides at W717 Nora Avenue, broke her ankle when a child. In endeavoring to favor the broken ankle, the other ankle became diseased, and for fifty years she had suffered violently. She was instantly healed after she was ministered to at the healing rooms. She was also healed of ulcers of the stomach after twenty years of suffering.

Mrs. Miles Pearson, E2815 Illinois Avenue, suffered a broken ankle a year ago. It was not properly set and remained inflamed and swollen as though the leg would burst. She was healed in answer to prayer two weeks ago.

Mrs. Thomas Olsen, Rowan Street, healed when dying of internal cancer. For ten days she had touched neither food nor drink. A group of Christian friends gathered about her and prayed. As prayer was offered, Jesus appeared to her, standing in front of her, reaching out His hands appealingly. She endeavored to rise from her wheelchair and grasp the hands of her Lord, and as she did so, thrills of divine life flashed through her body, and she was healed. Two days later, she vomited the entire cancer, body and roots.

Mrs. Richards, Sandpoint, Idaho, testified that she had been healed when dying of tumors and paralysis on one side. After prayer, the tumors loosened and passed from the body.

Mrs. Allen of Waverly, rising in the audience with a friend who corroborated her testimony, was dying from internal cancers. She was brought to Spokane by Mr. Ramey, a hardware merchant of Waverly. She was perfectly healed and is now earning her living as a saleslady.

Mrs. Kellum, Portland, Oregon, testified to having been blind nine years. As prayer was offered, a vision of Jesus laying His hands upon her eyes appeared to her, and she was instantly healed.

❧◈❧

Addressing the audience, Mr. Lake said: "All persons who have been healed by the power of God and who desire to add their testimony to these who have already been given, stand." Two hundred and sixty-seven persons arose. While they stood, Mr. Lake said: "Gentlemen of the committee and audience, you see these witnesses, you have heard the testimonies. Gentlemen of the committee and audience, has this been a fair presentation?"

(Shouts of "Yes, Yes," from all parts of the house.)

"Did God heal these people?"

(Cries of "Yes, Yes!")

"Is divine healing a fact?"

(Replies from audience, "It surely is.")

"Gentlemen of the committee and audience, are you entirely satisfied?"

(Replies from the audience, "Indeed we are.")

The services then closed with the following prayer of consecration, spoken clause by clause by the Reverend Lake and repeated by the audience.

My God and Father,
In Jesus' name I come to Thee, take me as I am. Make me what I ought to be, in spirit, in soul, in body. Give me power to do right, if I have wronged any. To repent, to confess, to restore. No matter what it cost, wash me in the blood of Jesus, that I may now become Thy child and manifest Thee in a perfect spirit, a holy mind, a sickless body. Amen.

Chapter 16

The Word of God on Divine Healing

Sermon

1. Healing by God, through faith and prayer, was practiced by the patriarchs.

> *Abraham prayed unto God: and God healed Abimelech, and his wife, and his maidservants; and they bare children.* (Genesis 20:17)

2. God made a covenant of healing with the children of Israel. A covenant is an indissoluble agreement and can never be annulled. The laws of South Carolina recognized marriage as a covenant, not a legal contract. Therefore, in that state there is no divorce. A covenant cannot be annulled, as the unchangeable God is one of the parties. God tested the nation at the waters of Marah and made a *covenant* with them, known as the Covenant of *Jehovah-Rophi*, "The Lord thy Healer."

a. *If thou wilt diligently hearken to the voice of the* LORD *thy God,*

b. *and wilt do that which is right in his sight,*

> c. *and wilt give ear to his commandments,*
>
> d. *and keep all his statutes,...*

> *I will put none of these diseases upon thee, which I have brought upon the Egyptians.* **For I am the LORD that healeth thee.**   (Exodus 15:26)

3. David rejoiced in the knowledge of this covenant.

> *Bless the LORD, O my soul: and all that is within me, bless his holy name. Bless the LORD, O my soul, and forget not all his benefits: who forgiveth all thine iniquities; who* **healeth all thy diseases.**   (Psalm 103:1–3)

4. Isaiah proclaimed it.

> *Then the eyes of the blind shall be opened, and the ears of the deaf shall be unstopped. Then shall the lame man leap as an hart, and the tongue of the dumb sing.*
>
>   (Isaiah 35:5–6)

5. Jesus made healing one of the planks of His platform.

> a. *The Spirit of the Lord is upon me, because he hath anointed me to preach the gospel to the poor;*
>
> b. *he hath sent me to* **heal** *the brokenhearted,*
>
> c. *to preach deliverance to the captives,*
>
> d. *and recovering of sight to the blind,*
>
> e. *to set at liberty them that are bruised,*
>
> f. *to preach the acceptable year of the Lord.*
>
>   (Luke 4:18–19)

6. Jesus ministered healing to the sick.

> *And Jesus went about all Galilee, teaching in their synagogues, and preaching the gospel of the kingdom, and*

healing all manner of sickness and all manner of disease among the people. (Matthew 4:23)

7. Healing is in the atonement of Christ.

See Matthew 8:1–17.

a. Healing of the leper in Matthew 8:1–4.

b. Healing of the centurion's servant in Matthew 8:5–13.

c. Healing of Peter's wife's mother in Matthew 8:14–15.

d. Healing of the multitude in Matthew 8:16.

e. His reason given for these healings in Matthew 8:17: *"That it might be fulfilled which was spoken by Esaias the prophet, saying, Himself took our infirmities, and bare our sicknesses."*

8. Jesus bestowed the power to heal upon His twelve disciples.

Then he called his twelve disciples together, and gave them power and authority over all devils, and to cure diseases. And he sent them to preach the kingdom of God, and to heal the sick….And they departed, and went through the towns, preaching the gospel, and healing everywhere. (Luke 9:1–2, 6)

9. He likewise bestowed power to heal upon the seventy.

And after these things the Lord appointed other seventy also, and sent them two and two before his face into every city and place, whither he himself would come…. Heal the sick that are therein, and say unto them, The kingdom of God is come nigh unto you. (Luke 10:1, 9)

10. After Jesus' resurrection, He extended the power to heal to all who would believe.

> *He said unto them, Go ye into all the world, and preach the gospel to every creature. He that believeth and is baptized shall be saved; but he that believeth not shall be damned. And these signs shall follow them that believe, In my name shall they cast out devils, they shall speak with new tongues; they shall take up serpents; and if they drink any deadly thing, it shall not hurt them; they shall lay hands on the sick, and they shall recover.*
>
> (Mark 16:15–18)

11. And lest healing should be lost to the church, He perpetuated it forever as one of the nine gifts of the Holy Ghost.

> *For to one is given by the Spirit the word of wisdom; to another the word of knowledge by the same Spirit; to another faith by the same Spirit; to another the gifts of healing by the same Spirit; to another the working of miracles; to another prophecy; to another discerning of spirits; to another divers kinds of tongues; to another the interpretation of tongues.* (1 Corinthians 12:8–10)

12. The church was commanded to practice it.

> *Is any among you afflicted? let him pray Is any merry? Let him sing psalms. Is any sick among you? Let him call for the elders of the church, and let them pray over him, anointing him with oil in the name of the Lord: and the prayer of faith shall save the sick, and the Lord shall raise him up; and if he have committed sins, they shall be forgiven him. Confess your faults one to another, and pray one for another, that ye may be healed.*

The effectual fervent prayer of a righteous man availeth much. (James 5:13–16)

13. The unchangeableness of God's eternal purpose is thereby demonstrated.

Jesus Christ the same yesterday, and to day, and for ever. (Hebrews 13:8)

I am the LORD, I change not. (Malachi 3:6)

God always was the Healer. He is the Healer still, and will ever remain the Healer. Healing is for you. Jesus healed "all who came to him." (See Matthew 4:24, 8:16, 12:15, 14:14, 15:30, 19:2; Mark 1:34, 6:13; Luke 4:40, 6:19, 9:11.) He never turned anyone away. He never said, "It is not God's will to heal you," or that it was better for the individual to remain sick or that they were being perfected in character through the sickness. He healed them *all,* thereby demonstrating *forever* God's unchangeable will concerning sickness and healing.

Have you need of healing? Pray to God in the name of Jesus Christ to remove the disease. Command it to leave, as you would sin. Assert your divine authority and refuse to have it. Jesus purchased your freedom from sickness as He purchased your freedom from sin.

*His own self bare our sins in his own body on the tree, that we, being dead to sins, should live unto righteousness: **by whose stripes ye were healed**.* (1 Peter 2:24)

Therefore, mankind has a right to health as he has a right to deliverance from sin. If you do not have it, it is because you are being cheated out of your inheritance. It belongs to you. In the name of Jesus Christ, go after it and get it.

If your faith is weak, call for those who believe and to whom the prayer of faith and the ministry of healing have been committed.

(See also Psalm 91; Isaiah 35; Matthew 8 and 9; Mark 16; Luke 11; John 9; Acts 3, 4, 8, 9, 10, 26; 2 Corinthians 12 and 13.)

Chapter 17

Is God Able to Heal? Does God Ever Heal? Does God Always Heal? Does God Use Means in Healing?

~❖~

Pamphlet, Price: 50 cents
By John G. Lake, Overseer, The Church at Spokane

The Southern Association of Evangelists, who recently met at Hot Springs, Arkansas, in a convention, wrote as follows:

<u>Reverend John G. Lake</u>
<u>Spokane, Washington</u>

Dear Sir:

We are submitting the following questions to about twenty-five of the leading professors, preachers, and evangelists for reply and recognizing your extensive experience in the ministry of healing, trust that you will favor us with an early reply.

The questions are as follows:

First: Is God able to heal?
Second: Does God ever heal?
Third: Does God always heal?
Fourth: Does God use means in healing?

These questions were suggested to us through their having been used in a discussion of healing by Philip Mauro of Washington, D.C.

The Reply

The first question, "Is God able to heal?" coming as an inquiry from the Church of Christ in her varied branches, as represented by your association, which includes ministers and evangelists of almost every known sect, is a confession of how far the modern church has drifted in her faith from that of the primitive church of the first four centuries.

That this apostasy is true may be readily seen by a study of the New Testament, together with the writings of the Christian fathers of the first centuries. That Jesus Christ was the accepted and recognized Healer, and the *only* Healer (healing through His followers) in the church for the first four hundred years of the Christian era is the testimony of every first-rate student.

That Jesus Himself healed *all* who came to Him and that the apostles also, after His resurrection and after the outpouring of the Holy Spirit upon the church on the day of Pentecost, continued to do the same, is a New Testament fact.[9] It is also well known that the church fathers testified to the vast extent of the miracle-working power of Christ through His followers until the days of Constantine. The early Christians accepted Jesus as a Savior of spirit, soul, *and body.* His consecration of Himself to God as the pattern consecration for all Christians for all times is declared by many of the Christian writers.

---

[9] Jesus healed all: see Matthew 4:24, 8:16, 12:15, 14:14, 15:30, 19:2; Mark 1:34, 6:13; Luke 4:40, 6:19, 9:11. The apostles continued to heal: see Acts 3:1–8, 5:16, 8:7, 28:8.

With the establishment of Christianity as the state religion under Constantine, a flood of heathendom poured into the church, and the vitality of the faith in Christ as Savior and Healer disappeared. Hordes of unbelievers came into the church with a very slight knowledge of Christ, bringing with them many heathen customs and practices, some of which quickly predominated in the church. Among these was trust in *man* rather than *Christ* as Healer of the body.

That isolated saints of God and groups of Christians have trusted God exclusively, and proved Him the Healer, is found in the experience of the church in every century. Among those in modern times were the Huguenots of France, who excelled in their faith in God. Many of them were consciously baptized in the Holy Ghost, and history records that many of them spoke in tongues by the power of the Holy Spirit. The sick were healed through their faith in Jesus Christ and the laying on of hands. Many prophesied in the Spirit. In these things the Huguenots were a reproduction of the original New Testament church.

The Waldenses knew Christ as their Healer and recorded many instances of wonderful healings.

With the coming of Protestantism and the establishment of the great churches of the present day, little knowledge of Christ as the Healer existed. Protestantism was established on one great principle, the revelation of Martin Luther, his watchword and slogan, *"The just shall live by faith"* (Romans 1:17; Galatians 3:11; Hebrew 10:38)—not by works of penance, but through faith in the living, risen, glorified Son of God.

Isolated cases of healing are recorded by Luther, John Knox, Calvin, Zwingli, and others of the reformers.

With the birth of Methodism under John Wesley, a fresh impetus was given to the teaching of healing through faith in Jesus. Wesley records in his journal many instances of wonderful healings of the sick, of casting out of demons, and remarkable answers to prayer. Healing was recognized by Wesley as a possibility of faith. He apparently, however, failed to see that the healing of the body is definitely, certainly included in the atonement of the Lord and Savior Jesus Christ and is part and parcel of the common salvation.

The modern teaching of healing received a new impetus through Dorothea Trudel, a factory worker in one of the German provinces. Under her ministry many were healed, so that eventually the German government was compelled to recognize her healing institution at Mannendorf and license it.

During the present century, a great number of men have definitely taught and practiced the ministry of healing. Among the writers on the subject of healing, who are well-known in the Christian church, are A. J. Gordon, Dr. A. B. Simpson of the Christian and Missionary Alliance, and Reverend Andrew Murray of South Africa.

The Reverend Andrew Murray's experience in healing was as follows: He was pronounced incurable of a throat disease known as "preacher's throat" by many London specialists. In despair, he visited the Bethshan Divine Healing Mission in London, conducted by Dr. Bagster. He knelt at the altar, was prayed for by the elders, and was healed. He returned to South Africa and wrote and published a book on divine healing,[10] which was extensively circulated in the Dutch Reformed Church of South Africa, of which he was the recognized leading pastor.

---

[10] Originally entitled *Divine Healing*, this book is currently published by Whitaker House under the title *Healing Secrets*.

The effect of the book was to call the people's attention to the fact that Jesus was the Healer still. Great celebrations took place in the various churches of South Africa when Andrew Murray returned, a living example of Christ's power and willingness to heal.

In a short time, persons who had read of his ministry of healing made request to their pastors to be prayed for, so that they might be healed. In some instances, the pastors confessed that they had no faith and could not honestly pray with them for healing. Others made one excuse or another. Eventually, the people began to inquire what the trouble was with their pastors. Andrew Murray, the chief pastor, had been healed. He had written a book on healing. Members of the church throughout the land were praying through to God and finding Him their Healer still. But the preachers in general were confessing lack of faith.

So the circulation of the book became an embarrassment to them. Instead of humbly confessing their need to God and calling upon Him for that measure of His Spirit's presence and power that would make prayer for the sick answerable, they decided to demand the withdrawal of Andrew Murray's book from circulation in the church, and this was done. Although the truth of the teaching of divine healing, and the personal experience in healing of the Reverend Andrew Murray and hundreds of others through his ministry, and the ministry of believers in the church remained unchallenged, the Reverend Murray was requested not to practice the teaching of divine healing in the Dutch Reformed Church of South Africa.

This experience illustrates with clearness the difficulties surrounding the introduction of a more vital faith in the living God in the modern church. Every church has had, in a greater or lesser degree, a somewhat similar experience. The usual custom in the modern church is that when a preacher breaks out in a living faith and begins to get extraordinary answers to prayer, he is advised by the worldly-wise; and, if he is persistent, is eventually made to feel that he is regarded strange. If he still persists, he is ostracized and actually dismissed by some churches and conferences.

Experiences like the above are entirely due to the failure of the modern church to recognize the varied ministries of the Spirit, as set forth in the New Testament. In 1 Corinthians, the Word says concerning the order of ministers in the church that:

> God hath set some in the church, first apostles, secondarily prophets, thirdly teachers, after that miracles, then gifts of healings, helps, governments, diversities of tongues.
> (1 Corinthians 12:28)

Thus, a ministry for every man called of God is provided, no one conflicting with the other, all recognized as equally necessary to the well-rounded body of Christ.

The modern church must come to a realization of other ministries in the church besides preaching. In the modern church, the preacher is the soul and center and circumference of his church. The primitive church was a structure of faith composed of men and women, each qualifying in his or her particular ministry. One was a healer, another a worker of miracles, another a teacher of the ways and will and Word of God, another an evangelist, another a pastor, another an overseer.

It should be an easy matter for any modern church to adapt itself to the gifts of the Spirit and so remove forever the difficulty that befell the Dutch Reformed Church in South

Africa and that has befallen our own churches. Instead of discouraging a ministry of the Spirit through the practice of varied persons, these ministries and powers may be conserved and utilized for the building up of the kingdom.

Our neglect in this matter has forced into existence such institutions as Christian Science and one-thousand and one new thought societies and varied philosophies, which endeavor to supply that which in the primitive church was supplied through the Lord Jesus Christ and the ministry of spiritual gifts by His followers in the church.

Nevertheless, the knowledge of Jesus, the Healer now and forever, has spread among the masses of the people until in almost every city there are organized groups of Christian people who trust in God wholly and solely and proclaim Jesus their only Healer.

A new day is dawning, and knowledge of the reality and power of the redemption of Jesus Christ is recognized on every hand. A little over five years ago in Spokane, we established divine healing rooms, with a competent staff of ministers. They believe in the Lord as the present, perfect Healer, and they minister the Spirit of God to the sick through prayer and the laying on of hands. The records show that we minister to about two hundred persons per day; that of these two hundred, one-hundred seventy-six are non-church members. The knowledge of and faith in Jesus Christ as the Healer has gripped the world outside of the present church societies, and the numbers of those who thus believe are increasing with such rapidity that in a short time, they will become a majority in many communities.

These healings have been of the most extraordinary character, as shown by the fact that great numbers of them have been declared incurable by physicians and surgeons, proving the fallacy of the oft repeated foolish statement that "the days of miracles are past." It demonstrates that the day of miracles never passes where faith is present to believe God for the thing declared in His Word.

A boy of twelve years, suffering from tuberculosis of the spine so extreme that he was compelled to wear a steel jacket both day and night, was brought to the healing rooms a few days ago for prayer. In less than ten days, his condition was so improved that he discarded the jacket entirely; his shoulders had straightened, and his vertebrae remained fixed. The boy, James Early, returned to his home at Rosalia, Washington, praising God that he had proven that in our own city in March 1919, Jesus Christ is still the Healer.

Another Incident

We ministered to Grover Risdon of 914 Rockwell Avenue, Spokane, and God performed one of the most remarkable miracles of healing that is known to history. When Baby Grover was born, he was found to have a closed head; the opening in the top of the head that permits the skull to expand was closed. The brain grew, forcing the skull upward three inches, like the ridge of a house roof. The forehead was forced upward in the same manner and the back of the head likewise.

The pressure on the brain caused paralysis of the right side and leg, also the foot. The child was dumb. Medical science could give no relief or offer a cure. Surgical science said, "Wait until he is twelve years old; then we will cut the skull into eight sections and put a plate over the head to cover the brain." Surgeons frankly said, "We fear such an operation may destroy his life, but it is his only chance."

Then the parents, in distress, turned to the church and pastors, but they told them, "God does not hear prayer for healing now; that was to prove to the people in Jesus' day that He was divine."

The father said, "If He healed my stricken son, it would prove to me that He is divine *now*."

Then hope came. The mother suffered with prolapse of the uterus. She came to the healing rooms and was healed. *Faith grew.*

Her daughter, Alice, was partially blind and could only see by the use of the most powerful glasses. She was stricken with appendicitis. When she was suffering tortures, holy hands were laid upon her in Jesus' name, and she was healed.

Then Grover was brought to the healing rooms. As we ministered to him the second time, the paralysis was destroyed. He could walk like other children. Then the head began to come down and expand normally; and in a short time, he could speak like other six-year-old children.

God's work is perfect. He is wholly well. And the boy, his parents, his family, the neighborhood, the city of Spokane, and the world are better because Jesus Christ was honored as Savior and Healer still.

Thousands healed by God's power in the city of Spokane and the surrounding country join with them, proclaiming that they, too, have proved the Lord Jesus Christ—"*The same yesterday, and to day, and for ever*" (Hebrews 13:8)—Savior and Healer.

This letter is respectfully submitted as an answer to your question, "Is God able to heal?" For Jesus said, "*If I do [the works of My Father],…though ye believe not me, believe the* works" (John 10:38). He also said, "*Is it easier to say to the sick of the palsy, Thy sins be forgiven thee; or to say, Arise, and take up thy bed, and walk?*" (Mark 2:9).

Does God Ever Heal? *yes*

The New Testament records forty-one cases of healing by Jesus Himself. In nine of these instances not only were the individuals healed, but multitudes, and in three instances it especially says "*great multitudes*" (Matthew 12:15; 15:30; 19:2).

With the growth of His life's work, the demand for extension was imperative, and in Luke 9, we read:

> He called his twelve disciples together, and **gave them power** and authority over all **devils**, and to cure **diseases**. And he sent them to preach the kingdom of God, and to **heal the sick**.   (Luke 9:1–2)

When they in turn were overwhelmed with work, we read that Jesus appointed seventy others also, and sent them into the cities round about, saying, "*Heal the sick that are therein, and say unto them, The kingdom of God is come nigh unto you*" (Luke 10:9).

If there was any foundation whatever for the foolish belief that only Jesus and the apostles healed, the appointment of these seventy should settle it. When the seventy returned from their first evangelistic tour, they rejoiced, saying, "*Lord, even the devils are subject unto us through thy name*" (Luke 10:17).

In addition to the seventy, we read that the disciples complained to Jesus, saying, "*We saw one casting out devils in thy name; and we forbad him, because he followeth not with us*" (Luke 9:49). And Jesus replied, "*Forbid him not: for there is no man which shall do a miracle in my name, that can lightly speak evil of me....He that is not against us is for us"* (Mark 9:39; Luke 9:50).

This, then, makes a New Testament record of eighty-four persons who healed during the lifetime of Jesus. Jesus, the twelve apostles, seventy others, and the man who *"followeth not with us."*

Paul and Barnabas were not apostles during the lifetime of Jesus, but we read in the Acts of their healing many. Paul himself was healed through the ministry of Ananias, an aged disciple who was sent to him through a vision from the Lord. (See Acts 9.)

Philip was one of the evangelists who preached at Samaria, and under his ministry there were remarkable signs and wonders. (See Acts 8:13.)

Under the ministry of the apostle Paul, the sick were not only healed and the dead raised, but also handkerchiefs were brought to the apostle that they might contact his person. When laid upon the sick, the diseases disappeared, and the evil spirits departed from them. (See Acts 19:12.)

The book of James gives final and positive instructions of what to do in case of sickness, commanding that, if sick, one shall send for the elders of the church. Concerning their prayer of faith, the Word says,

> *The prayer of faith shall save the sick, and the Lord **shall raise him up**, and if he have committed sins, they shall be forgiven him.* (James 5:15)

Forty years after Jesus, Clement, Paul's contemporary, said, "Men received gifts of healing." Irensaus, a hundred and ten years after Christ, said, "Men healed the sick by laying their hands upon them."

Justin Martyr (AD 110–163) wrote concerning the operation of God in the church in his day, "For one receives the spirit of understanding, another of council, another of strength, another of healing, another of teaching, and another of the fear of God." And again he said, "For many demoniacs throughout the whole world and your city, many of our Christian men exorcising them in the name of Jesus Christ, who was crucified by Pontius Pilot, have healed and do heal."

Two hundred years after Christ, Origen wrote, "Men had marvelous power of curing by invoking the divine name. They expel evil spirits and perform many cures and foresee certain events, according to the will of the Logos."

St. Ambrose, Bishop of Milan (AD 340–397) tells of one Severne, a butcher by business, who became blind and was healed of the Lord.

It is recorded of St. Macarius of Alexandria (AD 375–390),

> A man withered in all his limbs and especially in his feet was anointed in the name of the Lord, and when commanded in the name of the Lord Jesus Christ, "arise, and stand on thy feet, and return to thy house," immediately arising and leaping, he blessed God.
>
> …There was brought to him from Thessalonica a noble and wealthy virgin, who for many years had been suffering from paralysis. With his own hands he anointed her, pouring out prayer for her to the Lord and so sent her back cured to her own city.

St. Augustine (AD 426) declared, "But the miracles that persons ascribed unto their idols are in no way comparable to the wonders wrought by our martyrs."

In AD 698, a man named Bethwegan, paralyzed on one side, prayed at the tomb of Cuthbert: "In the midst of his prayer he fell, as it were, into a stupor...felt a large hand touch his head where the pain lay....He was delivered from the weakness, restored to health down to his feet He rose up in perfect health, returning thanks to God for his recovery." It is said that the very garments that St. Cuthbert had worn during life remained so impregnated by the divine Spirit of God that, like the handkerchiefs taken from Paul's body to the sick, the virtue from his garments cured many, as may be seen in the book of his life and miracles.

Medieval history records miracles of healing having taken place at the following shrines: those of St. Thomas at Canterbury, Our Lady at Walsingham, St. Edward the Confessor at Westminster, St. William at York, St. Cuthbert at Durham, St. Thomas at Hereford, St. Osmund at Salisbury, St. Erkenwald at London, St. Hugh at Lincoln, St. Wulfstan at Worcester, Little St. William at Norwich, St. Werburgh at Chester, and St. Frideswide at Oxford.

In this connection, may we say that in the canonization of saints it was necessary to establish before a court the fact that, in at least two instances, actual miracles had been performed. In this connection we quote, "The evidence was sifted to the utmost and every disqualifying feature was made the most of." So the Pope Benedict XIV had a right to say, "The degree of proof required is the same as that required for a criminal case."

These medieval miracles, therefore, deserve respectful treatment, and the cumulative evidence of so much concurrent testimony by distinguished and upright men makes it impossible to think that they were all deluded and mistaken.

Among those canonized, and others in whose lives there was positive evidence of the healing power of Christ in well-established cases, are (according to Bede): St. John of Beverly (AD 721), St. Bernard (AD 1091–1153), St. Francis of Assisi (AD 1182–1226), St. Thomas of Hereford (AD 1282–1303), St. Catherine of Siena (AD 1347–1380), Martin Luther (AD 1483–1546), St. Francis of Xavier (AD 1506–1552), St. Phillip Neri (AD 1515–1595), Pascal's niece (AD 1646), George Fox (AD 1624–1691), John Wesley (AD 1703–1791), Prince Hohenlohe (AD 1794–1847), Father Matthew (AD 1790–1856), Dorothea Trudel (AD 1813–1862), Johann Blumhardt (AD 1805–1880), and Father John of Cronstadt (AD 1829–1908).

Concerning the reliability of the present existence of the miracle-working power of God, permit me to quote Richard Holt Hutton, justly estimated as one of the broad-minded writers and who was regarded as a profound materialist. "But whatever miracles be, history shows a great amount of evidence…that such events have happened in all ages.… Enthusiasm and fraud cannot be asked to account for as much evidence on this subject as exists."

It is a matter of common knowledge that ten thousand persons were healed under the ministry of Dorothea Trudel of Mannendorf.

The records of the Russian courts show that such a multitude of persons where healed under the ministry of Father John of Cronstadt, who died in 1908, that the church of Russia, fearing his growing and powerful influence, decided to have him imprisoned. Because of the great numbers who were healed under his ministry and who became his faithful adherents, and because of his extreme age, they decided that it was wiser to let him live out his natural life than to undertake his control by the church.

During the life of John Alexander Dowie, before his mentality was affected through overwork, he established a city in the state of Illinois, forty miles north of Chicago on the lakeshore, known as Zion City. This city was established in 1901. In twelve months it had a population of four thousand. In three years the population was estimated to be ten thousand. The city council passed by-laws banishing forever doctors, drugs, medicines, and use of swine's flesh. None of these are used by his followers if they wish to remain in good standing.

Their vital statistics reveal that their death rate is lower than that of other cities of the same population. Insurance companies were afraid to insure the Zion people because of the well-known fact that they would not employ physicians or take medicines. But at present, insurance companies are seeking their business. They are now recognized to be among the healthiest people in the United States.

On an occasion at the Chicago Auditorium, persons from all parts of the world who had been healed through their ministry were invited to send testimonies on a card two-and-a-half by four-and-a-half inches. It required five bushel baskets to hold these cards. They numbered sixty thousand. Ten thousand persons in the audience rose to their feet, testifying to their own personal healing by the power of God, making a grand total of seventy thousand testimonies.

In South Africa, divine healing now holds such sway among both black and white that army officers estimated that in the recent war, twenty out of every hundred [servicemen] refused medical aid and trusted God only. This necessitated in the army the establishment of the Divine Healing Corps, who ministered healing by the Spirit of God.

By the most careful estimates The Church at Spokane reports one hundred thousand healings in the past five years. Spokane has become celebrated as the greatest divine healing center in the world.

The hotels of the city testify to the continuous supply of patients coming from all parts of the world to receive ministry, and among the healed are a goodly number of physicians who, like others, have found the Lord Jesus Christ is the True and Great Physician.

Among prominent physicians who have not only been healed of God, but who also have adopted the ministry of healing through faith in the Lord Jesus Christ are: Phineas D. Yoakum of Los Angeles, head of the Pisga Institution, whose blessed ministry of healing is recognized by Christians everywhere; Dr. William D. Gentry of Chicago, who not only was prominent in his profession as a physician, but also as the author of *Materia Medica* in twenty volumes, which is found in every first-class medical library (his publisher sold over one hundred thousand copies of this work); and Dr. A. B. Simpson, the founder and head of the Missionary and Christian Alliance, which is said to maintain a thousand missionaries in different parts of the world, is another former doctor under whose ministry miracles of healing have continuously occurred.

To this I add my personal testimony that, after twenty-five years in the ministry of healing, hundreds of thousands of sick have been healed of the Lord during this period, through churches and missionary societies founded on the pattern of the primitive church, finding God's divine equipment of power from on high.

With this weight of testimony before us, it seems childish to continue debating the ability or willingness of God to heal the sick. Let us rather, with open minds and heart, receive the Lord Christ as Savior and Healer, trusting Him with our bodies as we trust Him with our souls and so permit His hundredfold salvation for every need of the spirit, soul, and body to be exemplified and our consecration as the children of God stand unchallenged.

Does God Always Heal?

In considering the subject of divine healing and its applicability to present-day needs, the question, "Does God always heal?" is uppermost. The church at large has taught that healing is dependent on the exercise of the will of God and that the proper attitude for the Christian to assume is, "If it be Thy will." Continuously, we hear men say, "No doubt God can heal; He has powers, and He can heal if He will."

We believe that this attitude of mind and this character of reasoning are due to ignorance of the plain Word and will of God, as revealed through Jesus the Christ. We contend that God is always the Healer. We contend further that it is not necessary for God to will and that He does not will the healing or non-healing of any individual. In His desire to bless mankind, He willed once and for all and forever that man should be blessed and healed. He gave Jesus Christ as a gift to the world, so that this blessing might be demonstrated and His willingness and desire to heal forever made clear.

Christians readily admit that Jesus is the entire expression of the law, the life, and the will of God. As such, He demonstrated forever by His words and acts, what the mind of God toward the world is He healed all who came to Him, never refusing a single individual, but ever bestowed the desired blessing. In healing all and never refusing one, He demonstrated forever the willingness of God to heal all, both saint and sinner.

It is absurd to think that only the good were healed by Jesus. He healed *all* who came. (See Matthew 4:24, 8:16, 12:15, 14:14, 15:30, 19:2; Mark 1:34, 6:13; Luke 4:40, 6:19, 9:11.) Their coming was sufficient to secure the blessing. He healed because it was the nature of God to heal, not because it was a caprice of the mind of God, or not because the mind of God was changed toward the individual through some special supplication. Whosoever was ready and willing to receive healing received it from the Lord. His grief, in one instance, is expressed in the gospel narrative in that, "*He could there* [at Nazareth] *do no mighty work, save that he laid his hands upon a few sick folk, and healed them. And he* [was amazed] *because of their unbelief*" (Mark 6:5–6).

Men have assumed that it is necessary to persuade God to heal them. This we deny with all emphasis. God has manifested His desire to bless mankind through Christ.

> *For God so loved the world, that he gave his only begotten Son, that whosoever believeth in him should not perish, but have everlasting life. For God sent not his Son into the world to condemn the world; but that the world through him might be saved.* (John 3:16–17)

> *I am come that they might have life, and that they might have it more abundantly.* (John 10:10)

His method of saving the world—and what constituted His salvation—is shown in Matthew:

Jesus went about all Galilee, teaching in their synagogues
[revealing the will of God], and preaching the gospel of
the kingdom, and healing all manner of sickness and all
manner of disease among the people. (Matthew 4:23)

The facts of God's will, of His purpose to establish the kingdom of Christ, and of His deliverance from sickness—a kindred blessing for spirit and soul and body are here provided in the common salvation.

The redemption of Jesus does not rest on His crucifixion alone. It rests equally in a combined victory of crucifixion, resurrection, and ascension. Each step was an elevation in divine consciousness to one end, the bestowal of the Holy Spirit upon the world. Through His crucifixion, He fulfilled the type and fact of the Jewish sacrifice. (See Hebrews 9:26, 10:12.) Through His resurrection, He manifested and demonstrated His power over death and that death itself was made a captive. (See Romans 6:9; 2 Timothy 1:10; Revelation 1:18.) Through His ascension to the throne of God and through receiving from the Father, the gift of the Holy Ghost, He was now equipped to bestow universal salvation upon whosoever would receive. (See John 14:12–17; Acts 1:4–8, 2:38.)

The method by which men receive the healing power is parallel to the method by which we light our homes through the use of electricity. A dynamo is set up. Through its motion, it attracts to itself from the atmosphere the quality known as electricity. Having attracted electricity, it is then distributed through the wires wherever man wills, and our homes are lighted thereby. The dynamo did not make the electricity. It has been in the atmosphere from time immemorial. It was the discovery of the ability to control the electricity that made the lighting of our homes a possibility. Without it, we would still be living by the light of a tallow candle or a kerosene lamp.

In the spiritual world, the spirit of man is the dynamo. It is set in motion by prayer, the desire of the heart. Prayer is a veritable Holy Spirit-controlling dynamo, attracting to itself the Spirit of God. The Spirit of God being received into the spirit of man through prayer is distributed by the action of the will wherever desired. The Spirit of God flowed through the hands of Jesus to the ones who were sick and healed them. It flowed from His soul, wirelessly, to the suffering ones and healed them also.

The Holy Spirit is thus shown to be the universal presence of God—God omnipresent. The Spirit of God is given to man for his blessing and is to be utilized by him to fulfill the will of God.

The will of God to *save* a man is undisputed by intelligent Christians. The will of God to *heal* every man is equally God's purpose. God has not only made provision that, through the Spirit of God received into our lives, our souls may be blessed and our bodies healed, but further we in turn are expected and commanded by Jesus to distribute the Spirit's power to others, that they likewise may be blessed and healed. *"And these signs shall follow them that believe; in my name,"* said Jesus, *"...they shall lay hands on the sick, and they shall recover"* (Mark 16:17–18). This refers not to a special priest or a particular individual endowed with peculiar powers, but to the *believer*, the everyday man who accepts the gospel of Jesus Christ and who becomes a declared disciple of the Son of God. (See Mark 16:14–20.)

The Spirit of God is ours to embrace. It is ours to apply to the need of either soul or body. It is the redeeming quality of the nature of God that Jesus Christ regarded as essential to the world's blessing. His life on earth, His death on the cross, His resurrection from the dead, and His ascension to glory were all necessary to secure its benefits and bestow them upon the world. It was Christ's means of supplying a universal salvation for whosoever will accept it.

On the day of Pentecost, when the floodtide of the Holy Spirit broke over the church at Jerusalem and its glory-power radiated through their souls and rested upon them as tongues of fire and they were filled with the Holy Ghost and began to speak with other tongues as the *Spirit* gave them utterance, the people demanded an explanation of the phenomena. (See Acts 2:1–12.)

Peter replied,

> *This Jesus hath God raised up* [resurrection], *whereof we all are witnesses. Therefore being by the right hand of God exalted* [ascension], *and having received of the Father the promise of the Holy Ghost* [fulfillment of the promise of the Father], *he hath shed forth this, which ye now see and hear.* (Acts 2:32–33)

Through His crucifixion and through His victory over the grave, Jesus secured from the Father the privilege of shedding the Holy Spirit abroad over the world. This was the crowning climax of the redemptive power of God ministered through Jesus Christ to the world. And from that day to this, every soul is entitled to embrace to himself this blessed Spirit of God which Jesus regarded so valuable to mankind, so necessary for their healing and salvation, that He gave His life to obtain it.

Consequently, it is not a question, "Does God always heal?" That is childish. It is rather a question, "Are we willing to embrace His healing?" If so, it is for us to receive. More than this, it is for all the world to receive, for every man to receive who will put his nature in contact with God through opening his heart to the Lord.

Jesus, knowing the world's need of healing, provided definitely for physicians (disciples, ministers, priests, healers) who would minister, not pills and potions, but the *power of God*. The gift of healing is one of the nine gifts of the Spirit provided for and perpetuated forever in the church. (See 1 Corinthians 12:8–11.)

It is an evidence of ignorance of God's Word to continue to discuss the question, "Does God always heal?" as though God healed sometimes, and sometimes He did not. Enlightenment by the Spirit of God, through the Word, reveals that God always was the Healer, is the Healer today, will be the Healer forever. The Word says, *"Jesus Christ the same yesterday, and to day, and for ever"* (Hebrews 13:8). Consequently, there is healing from every disease for every man who will, in faith, embrace the Spirit of God promised by the Father and ministered through Jesus Christ to the souls and bodies of all who desire the blessing.

Peter, in his exposition of this fact said, *"By whose stripes ye **were** healed"* (1 Peter 2:24). The use of *"were"* in this text indicates that the healing was accomplished in the mind of God when Jesus Christ gave Himself as the eternal sacrifice and has never had to be done over again for the healing of any individual. He *willed* it once; it is done forever. He made the provision and invites the world to embrace it. It is yours to have, yours to enjoy, and yours to impart to others.

Does God Use Means in Healing?

By the term *means* is understood the varied remedies, medicines, and potions commonly used by the world at large and prescribed for the sick—in short, *materia medica.*[11]

This should be an extremely easy question for anyone to decide. The world has always had her system of healing. There were the thousand and one systems of healing evolved in all the centuries; these were mankind's endeavor to alleviate suffering. They existed in the days of Jesus, just as they exist today.

Systems of so-called healing are without number. The ancient Egyptians used them and were apparently as proficient in the practice of the same as our modern physicians. Indeed, their knowledge of chemistry seems to have superseded ours, as they were able to produce an embalming substance that preserved the human body and kept it from dissolution, for almost every museum of note has its samples of Egyptian mummies.

It is the unintelligent who suppose that the ancient physicians were any less skillful in the healing of the sick through their means, remedies, and systems than the modern physician.

Of the supposed curative value of our modern medical practice, there is an abundance of testimony from the varied heads of the medical profession that should be sufficient to convince any candid thinker of their valuelessness:

+ The public commonly believes that medicine is a science and that its practice is entirely scientific. Whereas, so great a man as Professor Douglas

---

[11] *materia medica:* substances used in the composition of medical remedies: drugs, medicine; a branch of medical science that deals with the sources, nature, properties, and preparation of drugs. *Merriam-Webster's 11th Collegiate Dictionary* CD-ROM, © 2003.

McGlaggen, who occupied the chair of medical jurisprudence in the University of Edinburgh, Scotland, declared, "There is no such thing as the science of medicine. From the days of Hippocrates and Galen until now we have been stumbling in the dark, from diagnosis to diagnosis, from treatment to treatment, and have not found the first stone on which to found medicine as a science."

+ Mr. James Mason Good of London, England, who was so eminent in his profession that for twenty-five years he had in his care the royal house of Britain, declared his convictions before the British Medical Association in these words, "The science of medicines is founded upon conjecture and improved by murder. Our medicines have destroyed more lives than all the wars, pestilences, and famines combined."

+ The famous Professor Chauss of Germany states with emphasis, "The common use of medicines for the curing of disease is unquestionably highly detrimental and destructive and, in my judgment, is an agent for the creation of disease rather than its cure, in that through its use, there is continuously set up in the human system abnormal conditions more detrimental to human life than the disease from which the patient is suffering."

+ Our own Dr. Holmes of Boston, formerly president of the Massachusetts Medical Association, said in an address before the Massachusetts Medical Association, "It is my conviction, after practicing medicine for thirty-five years, that if the whole *materia medica* were cast into the bottom of the sea, it would be all the better for mankind and all the worse for the fishes."

+ Dr. John B. Murphy, the greatest surgeon our country has ever produced, has spoken his mind concerning surgery as follows, "Surgery is a confession of help-lessness. Being unable to assist the diseased organ, we remove it. If I had my life to live over again, I would endeavor to discover preventative medicine, in the hope of saving the organ instead of destroying it."

Just prior to his death he wrote an at article entitled, "The Slaughter of the Innocents," condemning cutting out of tonsils and adenoids, demonstrating that the presence of inflammation and pus and the consequent enlargement was due to a secretion in the system that found lodging in the tonsils and that the removal of the tonsils in no way remedied the difficulty, the poison being generated in the system. He purposed to give his knowledge to the public for their protection from useless operations that he regarded as criminal.

From these quotations from the heads of the medical profession in various countries, we perceive the power of the Word of God, which declares, "*In vain shalt thou use many medicines* ["*In vain have you multiplied remedies,*" NASB]; *for thou shalt not be cured*" (Jeremiah 46:11).

God's Way in Contrast to Man's Way

What then, did Jesus have in mind as better than the world's systems of healing, which He never used or counte-nanced? God's remedy is a person, not a thing. The remedy that Jesus ministered to the sick was a spiritual one. It was the Holy Spirit of God. The tangible, living quality and nature of the living God, ministered through the soul and hands of Jesus Christ to the sick one.

So conscious was the woman who was healed of the issue of blood that she had received the remedy, and of its effect and power in her upon only touching the hem of His garment, that she "*felt in her body that she was healed of that plague*" (Mark 5:29). Jesus likewise was aware of the transmission of the healing power, for He said, "*Someone hath touched me, for I perceive that virtue has gone out of me*" (Luke 8:46).

This same virtue was ministered through the hands of the apostles and of the seventy. It was also ministered by the early Christians when they received from God, through the Holy Ghost, the ability to minister the Spirit of God to others. Of the twelve apostles, it is said:

> He gave them power and authority over all devils, and to cure diseases. And he sent them to preach the kingdom of God, and to heal the sick. (Luke 9:1–2)

Of the seventy, it is written that Jesus "*sent them two by two…into every city and place, whither he himself would come*" (Luke 10:1), and He said unto them, "**Heal the sick that are therein**, *and say to them, the kingdom of God is come nigh unto you*" (verse 9).

So vital was this living Spirit of God and its healing virtue in the lives of the early Christians that it is recorded of Paul that they brought handkerchiefs and aprons to him, that they might touch his body; and when these were laid upon the sick, they were healed and the demons went out of them. (See Acts 1:9.) In this instance, even inanimate objects, handkerchiefs and aprons, were receptacles for the Spirit of God, imparted to them from the Holy Spirit-filled person of the apostle Paul.

This was not an experience for the early Christian alone, but is the common experience of men and women everywhere who have dared to disbelieve the devil's lie—which is so carefully fostered and proclaimed by the church at large—that the days of miracles are past.

Every advanced Christian who has gone out into God, who has felt the thrill of His Spirit, who has dared to believe that the Son of God lives by the Spirit in his life today, just as He lived in the lives of the early Christians, has found the same pregnant power of God in himself. Upon laying his hands in faith upon others who are sick, he has seen with his own eyes the healing of the sick take place and realized the transmission of divine virtue. Today, millions of men and women trust God only, for the healing of their body from every character and form of disease.

What, then, is this means of healing that Jesus gave as a divine gift to Christianity forever? It is the living Holy Spirit of God, ministered by Jesus Christ to the Christian soul, transmitted by the Christian because of his faith in the word of Jesus, through his soul and his hands to the one who is sick. This reveals the law of contact in the mind of Jesus when He gave the commandment: *They shall lay hands on the sick, and they shall recover*" (Mark 16:18).

With praise to God, we record to His glory that, through twenty-five years in this ministry, we have seen hundreds of thousands of persons in many parts of the world healed by the power of God. Throughout these twenty-five years in different lands, we have established churches and societies composed of Christian men and women who know no remedy but the one divine remedy, the Lord Jesus Christ. They have faith in His redemption and in the presence and power of the Spirit of Christ to destroy sin and sickness in the lives of men forever.

In our own city, for five years, no day has passed in which we have not seen the healing of many. For five years we have ministered, with our associate pastors, in The Church at Spokane alone, to an average of two hundred sick per day, who come from all quarters of the land and even from foreign countries, to receive the healing power of God. These healings have included almost every known form of disease.

The majority of these healings have been of persons pronounced hopeless by their physicians. Many of them had spent their all, some tens of thousands of dollars, for doctors, medicines, and operations. They found the Lord Jesus Christ and the ministry of healing by the power of God just as efficacious today as it ever was, thereby demonstrating the truth of the Word of God.

Consecration Prayer

My God and Father,
In Jesus' name I come to Thee. Take me as I am. Make me what I ought to be in spirit, in soul, in body. Give me power to do right. If I have wronged any, to repent, to confess, to restore—no matter what it costs. Wash me in the blood of Jesus, so that I may now become Thy child and manifest Thee in a perfect spirit, a holy mind, and a sound body, to the glory of God. Amen.

Chapter 18

"Peace Be to This House"... and Why

~◦≍✦≍◦~

Sermon

*The Lord appointed other seventy also, and sent them
two and two before his face into every city and place,
whither he himself would come....And into whatsoever
house ye enter, first say, Peace be to this house.*
—Luke 10:1, 5

B ecause our Lord Himself would come to every home,
the Seventies [ministry team] of The Church at Portland, 129 Fourth Street (third floor), are going to every home in Portland with this message:

+ First, to save from sin.
+ Second, to heal from all sickness.
+ Third, to lead you into the way of holiness; to save
  you and yours body, soul, and spirit, both in this life
  and the one to come.

Preachers everywhere say that the Lord will save you
from sin, or at least from the consequences of it. Yet, when

235

it comes to the ailments of the body or, in fact, anything at all that is tangible or subject to demonstrable proof of any kind, they stand aloof, if indeed, they do not openly deny it. Sometime, somewhere, somehow, in some indeterminate place or state at a future time, when and where nobody in creation can tell, God is ready to do something—nobody knows what or how—but as to any real vital ministry to present-day necessities, there is almost none of it.

If Christianity is not a real, vital ministry to real, vital needs of today, it is not worth considering. But it is. And because we know that it is and that it is even more than we have claimed or can claim for it, we are vitally concerned to have all men everywhere made acquainted with it.

We speak not only from the Word of God but from experimental knowledge. We have put it to the test—not once, not a hundred times, but scores of thousands. It is of daily occurrence. Just a list of the names of those who have received healing and other helps through the prayers of the members of this church would fill a good sized book. Here are a few of the cases.

What the Lord Is Doing among Us Every Day

From the recent testimonies given in Dr. Lake's Thursday 3:00 PM divine healing meetings:

- *Mrs. Musselwhite*, Goodenough Building: I was almost blind. My physicians said they could not help me; I would be blind. Dr. Lake ministered to me through prayer and the laying on of hands, and the Lord restored my sight and healed the disease, and I can see to read now. Praise God.

- *Joseph Maplethorpe*, foreman of Portland Woolen Mills, St. Johns, Oregon: I was stricken with very death. Sixteen doctors had given up my case. I was in the agonies of hell. Mine was not just a healing of disease. I was veritably raised from the dead. As prayer was offered, Jesus appeared to me and put His arms about me, saved my soul and healed my body.

• *Miss Nelson*, professional nurse: The aperture to my stomach began to close. My doctors did their best, but could not heal me. I was in a sanitarium for months. Then I came here through the influence of friends, and the blessed Lord healed me entirely. I am sound and well and working every day.

• *Mrs. Copeland:* I have just been healed of a terrible inward goiter that was strangling me to death. I desire to tender praise to God for my healing and to thank Dr. Lake and all the dear people of this church who prayed so earnestly for my healing.

• *Mrs. Ida laVeres,* 1610 Chautauqua Street: I suffered with appendicitis. My doctor ordered my room arranged for an operation and sent the ambulance for me. My nurse advised me to send for Dr. Lake, as she had herself been healed through prayer. He prayed; the Lord healed me. The ambulance came to the door, but I was healed and am in perfect health. And best of all, I found my Lord and Savior Jesus Christ, to me, both Savior and Healer evermore.

• *Mrs. Herndon:* I was born with a crooked back, almost a hunch back. I developed a tumor of the bladder when I was forty-six years old. I was instantly healed of this tumor when Dr. Lake prayed. My back snapped five times as hands were laid on me in prayer, and in one minute, I was straight as I am today. How I love to praise God for it all.

These are only a few representative cases. We cite them not to show what hairsplitting doctrinal questions we might raise, but what is actually being accomplished in this day and generation in the city of Portland, and we can multiply them a thousand times.

We believe in a gospel that can be demonstrated, and we prove it.

The Poor Have the Gospel Preached to Them

This is what we are doing daily; going about among the poor and the lame and the halt and the blind, sin-stricken and disease-smitten, ministering God's love and power, fulfilling once more the declaration of Jesus, concerning the mark and stamp of real Christianity: "*The poor have the gospel preached to them*" (Matthew 11:5).

These Signs Shall Follow Them That Believe

In my name shall they cast out devils; they shall speak with new tongues; they shall take up serpents; and if they drink any deadly thing, it shall not hurt them; they shall lay hands on the sick, and they shall recover.

(Mark 16:17–18)

Chapter 19

Letter to the Editor, *Spokane Daily Chronicle*

❧◈❧

Letter
Addressed to Editor, *Spokane Daily Chronicle*

I n the *Spokane Daily Chronicle* of January 17th, there appeared a condensed report of a sermon by the Reverend F. E. Beattey of the Lidgerwood Presbyterian Church. The article is headlined "Healing by Faith Can't Be Expected." The article presents so much absurdity that it is difficult to imagine that it was actually delivered to an intelligent congregation.

The reverend gentleman stated that Jesus said to His disciples, *"As my Father hath sent me, even so send I you"* (John 20:21).

"Jesus' work may be summed up under three general headings: preaching, teaching, and healing," he says. "The church, therefore, is to preach the truths of eternal salvation and eternal punishment; teach the Word of God that men may know the Scriptures, which will make them wise unto salvation; and also make known the fact that the sick are not to be neglected."

He states the fact of Jesus' ministry as teaching and preaching and healing. He quotes the words of Jesus, *"As the Father hath sent me, even so send I you."* Nobody with sense could imagine that the disciples were sent to do anything else than what Jesus had done, in the manner He had done it. Is the disciple going to accomplish by another method different from the method of Jesus, the thing Jesus sent him to do? If the sick are to be healed, then we must discover how Jesus healed and how the disciples healed. In Luke 9:1–2, we distinctly read that *"He called his twelve disciples together, and gave **them** power and authority over all devils, and to cure diseases. And he sent them to preach the kingdom of God, and to heal the sick."*

He did not present them with a medicine kit. He sent them with the conscious power of God upon their lives, with spiritual dominion over sickness and demon powers. The Scriptures abound with healings through the ministry of the apostles. There is no question in any intelligent mind as to what the method was in connection with the revival in the city of Samaria; it is distinctly recorded in Acts:

> *The people with one accord gave heed unto those things which Philip spake, hearing and seeing the miracles which he did. For unclean spirits, crying with loud voice, came out of many that were possessed with them: and many taken with palsies, and that were lame, were healed.*
>
> (Acts 8:6–7)

These healings took place, not at the hands of the original twelve, to whom the power had first been given, but now at the hands of a new disciple, Philip.

The reverend gentleman says further, "I believe in the power of prayer, and I believe that some have been healed through prayer. Paul, the greatest apostle of the early church, besought God for help because of an infirmity, but he was not healed or given relief." We would like to inquire what this statement is based upon. If we can read the Scriptures correctly, certainly Paul was healed. He had prayed three times. He was not healed the first time, not the second time, but he prayed the third time and declares that the Lord said to him, "*My grace is sufficient for thee*" (2 Corinthians 12:9).

Surely the grace of God is sufficient for every man. It was sufficient for Paul's need, too. The assertion that he was not healed is one of the centuries-old theological jokes. Does our reverend friend expect a 1916 audience to believe that Paul was not healed when he prayed?

Again, there is not the least evidence in the Scriptures that he needed any healing. What his "*thorn in the flesh*" (verse 7) was is a pure conjecture. One thing we know, Paul was not only healed when he was blind, through the laying on of the hands of Ananias, but that he himself healed others.[12] On his way to Rome when his ship was wrecked, he healed the father of the governor of the island, and many others. (See Acts 28:8.)

The assertion that he was not healed himself is almost as stale an argument as the reference to Luke as "*the beloved physician*" (Colossians 4:14). Jesus was a beloved physician too. So were the apostles. So is any man who brings healing to the sick. There is not the least evidence in the Scriptures that Luke ever owned a medicine kit in his life; and if he did, he most certainly left it behind him when he accepted the ministry and power of the Lord Jesus Christ.

Our land is filled with men who have been physicians and who have abandoned the practice for the better way and

---

[12] Paul healed: see Acts 9:17–18; Paul heals: see Acts 14:9–10, Acts 28:8.

method of the Lord Jesus Christ: Dr. Finnis B. Yoakum, of Los Angeles, California, one of the leading physicians of his city, abandoned the practice of medicine and adopted the ministry of healing through the prayer of faith and the laying on of hands, as the superior method; Dr. W. D. Gentry, of Chicago, a writer on diagnosis, whose twenty-volume treatise on the subject is found in every first-class library, abandoned his practice of medicine and for years has ministered in the name of Jesus, through the prayer of faith and laying on of hands as Jesus commanded; likewise Dr. A. B. Simpson of New York, a leading osteopath, abandoned his practice of medicine; and many others.

Each one of these "beloved physicians" no longer gives pills. They have graduated into the higher way.

What a strange thing it is when Christian ministers are found endeavoring to dodge the real issue of healing instead of building up faith in God. In many cases, they are among the first to endeavor to break it down and try to explain away by some cunning method the real plain facts of the Scriptures. How much more honorable it would be if ministers would acknowledge, as they should, that Christ has not changed, that faith is the same quality as it ever was, but that they do not possess it and so are not able to secure answers to prayer for the sick.

Reverend Andrew Murray, the head of the Dutch Reformed Church of South Africa, whose books are throughout all Christendom and who is generally recognized as one of the saints of this age, was dying of an incurable throat disease. The physicians of Africa gave him no hope. He came to London, England, but received no hope from the medical men there. He went to Bagster's Bethshan Divine Healing Home and was perfectly healed.

He returned to South Africa and wrote a book on the subject of healing, and it was placed on sale by the church. After a little while, the ministers of the Dutch Reformed Church discussed it in conferences. They said, "If we leave this book in circulation, the people will read it. Then the next thing we know, they will ask us to pray the prayer of faith that saves the sick, and we have not the faith to do it, and our jobs will be in danger." So it was decided to withdraw the book from circulation.

Why not give the people the light of the Scriptures? Let them know that Jesus is the Healer still and that He empowers men today through the Holy Spirit to heal the sick, just as He ever did. That the Spirit of God is not obtained through the church, but that it comes upon the soul of man, straight from God Himself, when his necessary hundredfold consecration is made.

Chapter 20

Have Christians a Right to Pray "If It Be Thy Will" Concerning Healing?

❧❈❧

Sermon

I purpose this afternoon to speak on this subject: Do Christians have a right to pray "If it be Thy will" concerning sickness and healing? Personally, I do not believe they have, and I am going to give you my reasons.

I am going to read a familiar portion of the Word of God. It is the Lord's Prayer as recorded in the eleventh chapter of Luke:

> *And it came to pass, that, as he was praying in a certain place, when he ceased, one of his disciples said unto him, Lord, teach us to pray, as John also taught his disciples. And he said unto them, When ye pray, say, Our Father which art in heaven, Hallowed be thy name. Thy kingdom come. Thy will be done, as in heaven, so in earth. Give us day by day out daily bread. And forgive us our sins; for we also forgive every one that is indebted to us. And lead us not into temptation; but deliver us from evil.* (Luke 11:1–4)

Beloved, if there is one thing in the world I wish I could do for the people of Spokane, it would be to teach them to pray. Not teach them to say prayers, but teach them to pray. There is a mighty lot of difference between saying prayers and praying.

> *The prayer of **faith** shall save the sick, and the Lord shall raise him up; and if he have committed sins, they shall be for given him.* (James 5:15)

The prayer of faith has power in it. The prayer of faith has trust in it. The prayer of faith has healing in it for soul and body. The disciples wanted to know how to pray real prayers, and Jesus said unto them, "*When ye pray, say, Our Father which art in heaven,…Thy will be done.*"

Everybody stops there, and they resign their intelligence at that point to the unknown God. When you approach people and say to them, "You have missed the spirit of the prayer," they look at you in amazement. But, beloved, it is a fact. I want to show it to you this afternoon as it is written in the Word of God. It does not say "if it be Thy will" and stop there. There is a comma after, not a period. The prayer is this: "*Thy will be done in earth, as it is [done] in heaven*" (Matthew 6:10). That is mighty different, is it not? Not merely "*Thy will be done.*"

"Let the calamity come. Let my children be stricken with fever or my son go to the insane asylum or my daughter go to the home of the feebleminded." That is not what Jesus was teaching the people to pray. Jesus was teaching the people to pray, "*Thy will be done in earth, as it is in heaven.*" Let the might of God be known. Let the power of God descend. Let God avert the calamity that is coming. Let it turn aside through faith in God. "*Thy will be done [here on] earth, as it is in heaven.*"

How is the will of God done in heaven? For a little time, I want to direct your thoughts with mine, heavenward. We step over there, and we look all about the city. We note its beauty and its grandeur. We see the Lamb of God. We do not observe a single drunken man on the golden streets, not a single man on crutches, not a woman smelling of sin.

A man came in the other day and was telling me what an ardent Christian he is. But after he left, I said, "Lift the windows and let the balance of the man out." Men ought to smell like they pray. We defile ourselves with many things.

A dear man came to me the other day in great distress. He said his eyes were going blind. The physician told him he had only a year of sight, perhaps less. As I endeavored to comfort him and turn his face toward God, I reverently put my hands on his eyes and asked God for Christ's sake to heal him; and as I did so, the Spirit of God kept speaking to my soul and saying, "Amaurosis[13]." I said, "What is *amaurosis?*"

As soon as I could get to the dictionary, I looked up the word to see what it is. It is a disease of the eyes, caused by the use of nicotine. That was what was the matter with the man. The Spirit of the Lord was trying to tell me, but I was too dull. I did not understand. I do not know what the man's name is, but the other day God sent him back to my office. As we sat together, I related the incident to him and said, "My brother, when you quit poisoning yourself, the probability is that you may not need any healing from God."

We defile ourselves in various ways. We go on defiling ourselves, and some people are able to stand the defilement

---

[13] *amaurosis:* partial or complete loss of sight occurring especially without an externally perceptible change in the eye. *Merriam-Webster's 11th Collegiate Dictionary* CD-ROM, © 2003; many medical reports of the late 1800s–early 1900s cite the observed link between nicotine and alcohol usage and amaurosis.

a long time and throw it off. Others are not able to. It poisons their systems and destroys their faculties. One man may drink whiskey and live to be an old man. Another may go to wreck and ruin in a few months or years. Some systems will throw off much, others will not.

Now, when we get to the beautiful city and we don't find any of these conditions, we might say, "Angel, what is the reason you do not have any sin up here?"

"Why, the reason we do not have any sin here is because the will of God is being done."

I have been used to looking for the sick, and if I see a man with a lame leg or a woman with a blind eye, I will see them way down the street. I have mingled with the sick all my life. So I look around up there, and I do not see anybody on crutches or anybody that is lame, no cancers or consumption, or any sickness at all. So I say to my guide, "Angel, tell me what the reason is that you do not have any sickness up here."

The angel replies, "The will of God is being done here." There is no sin where the will of God is being done, no sickness where the will of God is being done.

Then I return to the earth, and I can pray that prayer with a new understanding. "Thy will be done in me on earth as Thy will is done in heaven." Just as the will of God is done there, so let the will of God be done here. Let the will of God be done in me. "*Thy will be done, as in heaven, so in earth*" (Luke 11:2).

But someone says, "Brother, do you not remember in the eighth chapter of Matthew how a leper came to Jesus one day and said to Him, '*Lord, if thou wilt, thou canst make me clean*' (Matthew 8:2)? When he prayed, the leper said, 'If it be Thy will.' Why should I not say that, too?" Well, he was ignorant of what the will of Christ was concerning sickness. Perhaps he had been up on the mountainside and had heard Jesus preach that wonderful sermon on the mount. For it was at its close that he came to Jesus and said, "*If thou wilt, thou canst make me clean.*"

He knew Christ's ability to heal but did not understand his willingness. Jesus' reply settled the question for the leper, and it should settle the question for every other man forever. Jesus said, "*I will, be thou clean*" (Matthew 8:3). If He ever had said anything else to any other man, there might be some reason for us to interject, "if it be Thy will," in our prayers when we ask God for something. He has declared His will on healing. *If* always doubts. The prayer of faith has no *ifs* in it.

Suppose a drunken man kneels down at this platform and says, "I want to find God. I want to be a Christian." Every man and woman in this house who knows God would say yes right away. "Tell him to pray, to have faith in God, and God will deliver him." Why do you do it? Simply because there is no question in your mind concerning God's will in saving a sinner from his sins. You know He is ready to do it when a sinner is ready to confess his sin. But you take another step over, and here is another poor fellow by his side with a lame leg, and he comes limping along and kneels down—or tries to—and right away a lot of folks say, "I wish he would send for a doctor," or they pray, "If it be Thy will, make him well," forgetting, "*who forgiveth all thine iniquities; who healeth all thy diseases*" (Psalm 103:3).

Instead of Christians taking the responsibility, they try to put the responsibility on God. Everything there is in the redemption of Jesus Christ is available for man when man will present his claim in faith and take it. There is no question in the mind of God concerning the salvation of a sinner. No more is there any question concerning the healing of the sick one. It is in the atonement of Jesus Christ, bless God. His atonement was unto the uttermost—to the last need of man. The responsibility rests purely, solely, and entirely on man. Jesus put it there.

Jesus said, *"What things soever ye desire,* **when** *ye pray,* **believe** *that ye receive them, and ye* **shall have** *them"* (Mark 11:24).

No questions or *ifs* in the words of Jesus. If He ever spoke with emphasis on any question, it was on the subject of God's will and the result of faith in prayer. Indeed, He did not even speak to them in ordinary words, but in the custom of the East, He said, *"Verily, verily."*[14] Amen, amen—the same as if I would stand in an American court and say, "I swear I will tell the truth, the whole truth, and nothing but the truth, so help me God." So the Easterner raised his hand and said, "Amen, amen," or "Verily, verily—with the solemnity of an oath, I say unto you." Thus, Jesus said, *"What things soever ye desire, when ye pray, believe that ye receive them, and ye shall have them."*

James, in expounding the subject, says concerning those that doubt, *"Let not that man think that he shall receive any thing of the Lord"* (James 1:7). Why? Well, he says, *"He that wavereth* [doubts] *is like a wave of the sea, driven with the wind and tossed"* (James 1:6). There is no continuity in his prayer. There is no continuity in his faith. There is no continuity in his character. There is no concentration in God for the thing that he wants. He is like the waves of the sea, scattered and shattered, driven here and there by the wind, because there is an *if* in it. *"Let not that man think he shall receive any thing of the Lord."*

---

[14] This phrase is used throughout the book of John.

Now that leper did not know what the mind of Jesus was concerning sickness. Perhaps he had seen others healed of ordinary diseases, but leprosy was a terrible thing. It was incurable and contagious. As he went down the road, the poor man was compelled to cry out, *"Unclean, unclean"* (Leviticus 13:45), in order that people might run away from him.

In my work in South Africa, I saw dozens of them, hundreds of them, thousands of them. I have seen them with their fingers off of the first joint, at the second joint, with their thumbs off or nose off, their teeth gone, the toes off, the body scaling off, and I have seen God heal them in every stage. On one occasion in our work, a company of healed lepers gathered on Christmas Eve and partook of the Lord's Supper. Some had no fingers on their hands, and they had to take the cup between their wrists, but the Lord had been there and healed them.

That was not under my ministry, but under the ministry of a poor, black fellow, who for five or six years did not even wear pants. He wore a goatskin apron. But he came to Christ. He touched the living One. He received the power of God, and he manifests a greater measure of the real healing gift than I believe any man ever has in modern times. And if I were over there, I would kneel down and ask that black man to put his hands on my head and ask God to let the same power of God come into my life that he has in his.

You have no more right to pray, "If it be Thy will," concerning your sickness than the leper had. Not as much, because for two thousand years the Word of God has been declared and the Bible has been an open book. We ought to be intelligent beyond any other people in the world concerning the mind of God.

"But Brother," someone says, "you have surely forgotten that when Jesus was in the garden, He prayed, '*O my Father, if it be possible, let this cup pass from me: nevertheless not as I will, but as thou wilt*'" (Matthew 26:39). No, I have not forgotten. You are not the Savior of the world, beloved. That was Jesus' prayer. No other man could ever pray that prayer but the Lord Jesus. But I want to show you, beloved, what caused Jesus to pray that prayer, because a lot of folks have never understood it.

Jesus had gone into the garden to pray. The burden of His life was upon Him. He was about to depart. He had a message for the world. He had been compelled to commit it to a few men—ignorant men. I believe that He wondered, "Will they be able to present the vision? Will they see it as I have seen it? Will they be able to let the people have it as I have given it to them?" No doubt these were some of the inquiries, besides many more.

Do you know what the spirit of intercession is? Do you know what it means when a man comes along, as Moses did, and takes upon himself the burden of the sin of the people and then goes down in tears and repentance unto God until the people are brought back in humility and repentance to His feet? When in anxiety for his race and people, Moses said, "Lord, if You forgive not this people, blot my name out of Your book!" (See Exodus 32:32.) He did not want any heaven where his people were not.

Think of it! Moses took upon himself that responsibility, and he said to God, "If You don't forgive this people, blot my name out of Your book." God heard Moses' prayer, bless God!

Paul, on one occasion, wrote practically the same words: "*For I could wish that myself were accursed from Christ for my* brethren, *my kinsmen according to the flesh*" (Romans 9:3). He felt the burden of his people. So in the garden, Jesus felt the burden of the world, the accumulated sorrows of mankind, their burdens of sin, their burdens of sickness. And as He knelt to pray, His heart breaking under it, the great drops of sweat came out on His brow like blood falling to the ground. But the critics have said, "It was not blood."

Judge V. V. Baines, in his great trial before Judge Landis, actually sweat blood until his handkerchief would be red with the blood that oozed through his pores. His wife said that for three months she was compelled to put napkins over his pillow. That is one of the biggest men God has ever let live in the world. His soul was big, and he saw the possibility of the hour for a great people and desired as far as he could to make that burden easy for them. He did not want the estate to go into the hands of a receiver. The interests of one hundred thousand people were in his hands, the accumulated properties of families who had no other resource. He was so large that the burden of his heart bore down on him, so that he was sweating blood, and did so for three months. But people of these days say, "It looked like blood," and are so teaching their Sunday school scholars. May the Lord have mercy on them! The blood came out and fell down to the ground.

Jesus thought He was going to die right there in the garden, but He was too big to die there. He wanted to go to the cross. He wanted to see this thing finished on behalf of the race of man, and so He prayed, *"Father, if it be possible, let this cup pass from me: nevertheless not as I will, but as thou wilt"* (Matthew 26:39). What was the cup? What is the cup of suffering that was breaking Him down, that was draining the life blood out right then, and that would be His death except the cross? But He towered above that and prayed, *"Father, if* it be possible, let this cup pass from me: nevertheless not as I will, but as thou wilt." Instantly, the angels came and ministered to Him; and in the new strength He received, He went to the cross and to His death as the Savior of mankind.

Beloved, I want to tell you that if there was a little sweating of blood and that kind of prayer, there would be less sickness and sin than there is. God is calling for a people who will take upon them that kind of burden and let the power of God work through them.

People look in amazement in these days when God answers prayer for a soul. A week ago last night, my dear wife and I went down to pray for a soul on the Fort Wright line, a Mrs. McFarland. She is going to be here one of these days to give her testimony. Ten years ago, a tree fell on her and broke her back. She became paralyzed, and for ten years she has been in a wheelchair, her limbs swollen and her feet great senseless lumps that hang down useless. She says many preachers have visited her in these years, and they have told her to be reconciled to the will of God, sit still, and suffer longer.

She said, "Oh, I would not mind not walking. If the pain would just stop for a little while, it would be so good." We lovingly laid our hands upon her and prayed. You say, "Did you pray, 'If it be Thy will'?" No! You bet I did not, but I laid my hands on that dear soul and prayed, "You devil that has been tormenting this woman for ten years and causing the tears to flow, I rebuke you in the name of the Son of God. And by the authority of the Son of God, I cast you out."

Something happened. Life began to flow into her being, and the pain left. In a little while, she discovered that power was coming back into her body. She called me up the other day and said, "Oh, such a wonderful thing has taken place. This morning in bed I could get up on my hands and knees." Poor soul, she called in her neighbors and relatives because she could get on her hands and knees in bed.

Do you know you have painted Jesus Christ as a man without a soul? You have painted God to the world as a tyrant. On the other hand, He is reaching out His hands in love to stricken mankind, desiring to lift them up. But He has put the responsibility of the whole matter on you and me. That question of the will of God was everlastingly settled long ago—eternally settled—no question about the will of God.

Bless God, the redemption of Jesus Christ was an uttermost redemption, to the last need of the human heart, for body, for soul, for spirit. He is a Christ and Savior even to the uttermost. Blessed be His name! Who shall dare to raise a limit to the accomplishment of faith through Jesus Christ? I am glad the tendency is to take down the barriers and let all the faith of your heart go out to God for every man and for every condition of life, to let the love of God flow out of your soul to every hungry soul.

Instead of praying, "Lord, if it be Thy will," when you kneel beside your sick friend, Jesus Christ has commanded you and every *believer* to lay your hands on the sick. This is not my ministry, not my brethren's only. It is the *ministry of every believer*. And if your ministers do not believe it, God have mercy on them; and if your churches do not believe it, God have mercy on them.

In these days, the churches are screaming and crying because Christian Science is swallowing up the world, and that it is false, etc. Why do the people go to Christian Science? Because they cannot get any truth where they are. Let the day come when the voices of men ring out and tell the people the truth about the Son of God, who is a Redeemer even unto the uttermost for body and soul and spirit. He redeems back to God. Beloved, believe it and receive the blessing that will come into your own life. Amen.

Chapter 21

Modes of Healing

∽⋘⋙∾

Sermon

There are four modes of healing, and more than that, but four principle modes taught in the Word of God. The first is the <u>*direct prayer of faith* of those,</u> who just like the leper, come to Jesus and say, *"Lord, if thou wilt, thou canst make me clean."* Jesus answered the leper, *"I will; be thou clean"* (Matthew 8:2–3; Mark 1:40–41; Luke 5:12–13). And His *"I will"* has rung down through the ages, for He healed *all* who came to Him. (See, for example, Matthew 4:24, 8:16; Luke 6:19.) He never turned one of them away. And in healing all that came to Him, He demonstrated forever what the will of God concerning sickness was.

"But, brother," you say, "are all the people healed whom you pray for?" No, they are not, and it is my sorrow; for I believe that if I was in the place before God where old Peter was and Paul was, bless God, all the people would be healed. And it is the purpose of my soul to let God take my soul into that place of real communion and consciousness of the power of God, through Jesus Christ, where all the people—not just some of the people—are healed.

However, beloved, I want to say that God made me too much of a man to try to dodge the issue and throw the responsibility off on God. My! How the church has worked at this acrobatic trick of throwing the responsibility over on God.

> *These signs shall follow them that believe:…they shall lay hands on the sick, and they shall recover.*
>
> (Mark 16:17–18)

Now, here is a sick man, and here comes the minister. As he gets close to him, the minister sees he is pretty bad. He is in trouble. He says to himself, "If I pray for him and he is not healed, the people will think I have not much faith in God." So he does the acrobatic trick and says, "It may not be the will of God that you should be healed." Do you see it?

How many did Jesus heal? *All* who came to Him; and in healing them all, He gave to mankind forever the finality concerning the will of God about healing the sick.

There is no further point to go in demonstration than Jesus went on the subject of the will of God. If He had ever turned one poor fellow away and said, "No, it is not God's will to heal you," then there could be a question mark set up; but having healed them all, He left the will of God concerning sickness forever settled and indelibly stamped forever on the human mind.

I am glad we know that kind of a Christ. An awful lot of people have been sent down the broad way through that old lie about the will of God and sickness.

"Well, brother," you say, "how are you going to get the people to heaven, if they are all healed? Why, they will live forever." Well, bless God, I am going one step further. However, we have not reached the place of faith yet where it is applicable in our lives. We are still discussing healing for the body.

Jesus said,

> Your fathers did eat manna in the wilderness and are dead. This is the bread which cometh down from heaven, that a man may eat thereof, and not die. I am the living bread which came down from heaven: if any man eat of this bread, he shall live for ever....And whosoever liveth and believeth in me shall never die. Believest thou this?
> (John 6:49–51, 11:26)

And many of His disciples turned away and walked no more with Him. (See John 6:66.) They said, "This is an hard saying; who can hear [receive] it?" (verse 60).

The faith of the church has never reached up to the place where we could dare to claim it. But beloved, I praise God that an ever-increasing number of men and women are rising up every day, who will enjoy stepping over the boundary into that hundredfold consecration, where they will consecrate once and forever their *bodies* and their *souls* and their *spirits* to God. Blessed be His name.

The consecration of the body to God is just as sacred as the consecration of the soul. No man can understand what the Christian life ought to be, what Jesus intended it to be, until the person sees the consecration that He made of Himself to the will of God. It is a pattern consecration for every other Christian. He was the first Christian, blessed be God. He consecrated His spirit to God, His soul to God, His body to God. Each was equally precious in the sight of God. Think of it!

Suppose that just once in His lifetime, when in trouble concerning the things of the Spirit, He had gone to the devil for help. Would He have been the spotless Lamb of God? Never! He would have been blemished. Suppose that in His mental distress, He had turned to the world for help and accepted the spirit of the world as His comforter. He would have been blemished in His soul life. He would not have been the spotless Lamb of God. Suppose one morning you would see the Lord Jesus sneaking around the back door into a drugstore to get ten cents' worth of pills for His body. Can you imagine such a thing? It is too horrible to imagine. If He had, He would never have been the spotless Lamb of God. He would have been blemished in His faith for His body before His Father.

But because the Christ demonstrated His power to trust God for His spirit, for His soul, and for His body, He became the author of eternal salvation and was able to present Himself to God a spotless conqueror and unblemished sacrifice.

And the hundredfold Christian, who received through the Holy Ghost the power of God and the dominion of the spirit, will present himself to God in the same manner—body and soul and spirit—unto God, a reasonable sacrifice and service. (See Romans 12:1.) Blessed be His precious name.

> *Know ye not that your body is the temple of the Holy Ghost which is in you?*   (1 Corinthians 6:19)

Shall I take this temple that I endeavor, by the grace of God, to lend to God for the purpose that He may dwell in my life by the Spirit, and fill it up with cocaine or digitalis or some of the other thousand and one damnable things that destroy human life and produce abnormal conditions in the system? Never, if I am a hundredfold child of God!

Here again is the ministerial acrobat with the gifts of the Holy Ghost.

> *To one is given by the Spirit the word of wisdom; to another the word of knowledge by the same Spirit; to another faith by the same Spirit; to another the gifts of healing by the same Spirit; to another the working of miracles, to another prophecy; to another discerning of spirits; to another divers kinds of tongues; to another the interpretation of tongues.*　　(1 Corinthians 12:8–10)

Paul said correctly that not all have these various gifts. That is perfectly correct. But beloved, the subject of gifts has nothing whatever to do with the principle of faith in God. The gifts are entirely extraordinary. The normal life of a real Christian with faith in God commands the power of God for his own need through *faith.* Have you ever noticed that the anointing with oil and the prayer of faith that saves the sick (see James 5:14–15) have nothing to do with the gifts of healing? It is an entirely different operation of healing. The elder or the priest comes in the name of Jesus. He anoints the man with oil and prays the prayer of faith. The prayer that expresses my faith in God that He will raise this man up is the *prayer of faith.* It is not the *gift of healing* at all, but simply the prayer of faith.

How far is it applicable? Jesus said,

> *If two of you shall agree on earth as touching any thing that they shall ask, it shall be done for them of my Father which is in heaven.*　　(Matthew 18:19)

The first healing I ever knew was the healing of a Roman Catholic girl who had formerly worked for my wife. Seven members in her family had died of consumption between the ages of eighteen and twenty-one. She was the last of the family. At the age of twenty, the disease appeared in her likewise. She was engaged to be married to a splendid fellow, but day by day she withered away, just as the others had done.

In those days I knew nothing about healing through God. A friend came to her and said, "Mary, let us observe a novena."[15] That is nine days of prayer. These two women, without any help from anyone, and who knew little or nothing of the Word of God, believing in the Christ as their Savior, began to pray throughout the nine days that God by His mighty power would raise the woman up. Her friend said, "When the Lord heals you, get up and come to my house." So on the ninth morning, when the time was complete and Mary did not appear at the friend's house, she got troubled and started down to see about it; and on the road, she met her coming. God had met the faith of two poor, simple women who had no teaching whatever on the subject of healing.

Among all the classes of people who come to our healing rooms, we find that Roman Catholics receive healing more readily than any other particular class of church people. You ask me why. They are educated to have faith in God. They are not educated to doubt Him. A great deal of modern preaching is an education in doubt concerning God. If you cannot explain the thing and you cannot demonstrate it, over you go, turn a somersault, and tell them it means something else.

A friend of mine in the city, who is a ministerial brother, used to be my pastor in the Methodist church when I was a <u>young man. He</u> was assistant pastor. Now he is one of the great

---

[15] *novena*: a Roman Catholic period of prayer lasting nine consecutive days. *Merriam-Webster's 11ᵗʰ Collegiate Dictionary* CD-ROM, © 2003.

ecclesiastical lights. I remember a sermon of his. He was ex-
plaining the fall of the walls of Jericho. Paul[16] wrote: *"By faith
the walls of Jericho fell down, after they were compassed about
seven days"* (Hebrews 11:30). *"By faith,"* by the united faith of
the people who dared to believe God, the very walls crumbled
and came down. Their instructions were to encircle the city
seven days and on the seventh day to go around it seven times;
and when the final march was completed, the priests, with
their trumpets and their rams' horns, were to sound a blast of
triumph to God, and the people were to give the shout of faith.
When they had sounded, the walls came down, *by faith*.

My friend very wisely said, "Every structure has a key
note, and if you just find and sound the key note of the structure, down it will come. The wise priests sounded the key
note and down the walls of Jericho came." That was his vision; Paul had a different one. He said, *"By faith the walls of
Jericho fell down, after they were compassed about seven days."*

Faith is not always characterized by beautiful phrases or
sweet prayers. I had a minister in my work in South Africa, a
very strong, vigorous man. He had a military training background; he was an officer in the army during the Boer war. His
name was W. I had another minister who was a nice, sweet,
gentle, tender man named J. He had none of the strong qualities
that W. possessed, but he loved God and had faith in Him.

One evening a Church of England minister sent in a call
about his wife, who was dying of a cancer. The doctors could
do nothing more, and now they wanted to trust God. That is
where a lot of people get to. May God almighty have mercy
on you. They are what we call "last resorters." We have an
expression among ourselves: "Is he a last resorter?"

---

[16] The apostle Paul has not been definitively determined to be the writer of Hebrews.

I reasoned that it would never do to send Brother W. down to that house, because he was such a strenuous man. He was likely to shock them. I said, "I will send Brother J. because he is one of those nice, polished men." So he went down and prayed for quite a long time. The rector knelt reverently at the foot of the bed and prayed with him, but there was no evidence of a real healing. After a while the telephone rang, and Brother J. was on the line. He said, "Brother Lake, I wish you would send W. down here; I cannot get the victory, and I need help."

I said, "Surely, I will." So I told Brother W. to go down and help him. He said, "All right, I will go," and away he started. When he arrived, he said, "What is the trouble, Brother J.?"

He said, "I do not know."

W. said, "Let us pray again." As he prayed, he said, "You damnable cancer, get to hell and out of here, in the name of Jesus Christ." The Spirit of God flamed in him, and the power of God fell on the woman. The cancer withered, and the woman was healed. After a while the telephone rang again. Brother J. said, "It is all right, Brother; she is healed, but the rector has not recovered from the effect of Brother W.'s prayer yet."

Bless God! There is something better than polished phrases. It is the faith of God that permits a soul to break through the darkness and the doubt that the devil and the world and the unbelieving church has heaped upon the souls of men.

It takes the power of God and the faith of God to break the bands that bind men's souls and get them through into the daylight of God. That is where healing, real healing, is found. I wish I could take a whole lot of you sick folks and get you broke through into the presence of God. You would not have to come to the healing rooms day after day if you did.

I have a conviction that there are mighty few Christian ministers who can tell you what divine healing is. In the world at large, I know there is a great deal of confusion. There is natural healing, medical healing, psychological healing, and there is divine healing. I am quoting my brother Beatty now. We recognize them all, but I want to tell you, beloved, the real Christian, the hundredfold Christian, the person who gives himself to God and receives the power of God, is not fooling around with medical healing, and not psychological healing either. They are good enough in their place, but God has given a better way and a higher way. There is as much difference between spiritual and psychological healing as there is between natural or medical and psychological healing. It is a higher plane and the higher life by a higher power, the power of God through the Holy Spirit.

Jesus demonstrated that to us so beautifully. He was walking down the road, and a poor woman, who had an issue of blood for twelve years, said within herself, *"If I may but touch his garment, I shall be whole"* (Matthew 9:21). You say that was faith. She could have had faith in a bread pill, because the doctors tell you if you have not faith in them, their drugs will do no good. You see, the virtue is not located in the remedy. It is in what you think of the doctor and your confidence in him. Every good doctor knows that fact.

It was not her faith in the sense we usually talk about faith. It was the virtue that was in Him. "If I could just touch the hem of His garment, I would be healed." How did she know it? Because she saw that those upon whom He laid His hands received virtue and were made whole. The virtue that was in Him flowed out and healed them. So she stole up in the crowd and touched the hem of His garment; and, bless

God, His very clothing was filled with the virtue of God, and it flowed from the garment to the woman, and she felt in her body that she was made whole, and Jesus felt it too.

Peter said, "Master, don't You see the multitude that is thronging You, and yet You say, 'Somebody touched me'?"

"Yes, but I perceive that virtue hath gone out of me." Hers was a different touch. It was the touch that received the life of the Christ into her own being. (See Luke 8:43-48.)

Divine healing is life, the life of God. Healing is transmitted into your being, whether it comes from heaven upon your own soul or is transmitted through a man of faith. It does not make any difference. It is the touch of the living Christ.

But you say, "Jesus was Jesus. Other men did not have that virtue."

Do you remember Paul, when they brought handkerchiefs and aprons in order that they might touch his body? (See Acts 19:12.) Then they were taken to the sick, and the sick were healed. Here is dear old Paul. A mother comes to him. "Oh, Paul, I have a sick boy at my house. He is dying of epilepsy, or typhoid fever, or cancer. Paul, here is my apron. Take it so that the Spirit of God will flow into it from your being." Then she takes the apron home with her and puts it on the boy, and the power of God that was in the apron flows out of it into the boy, and the boy is healed. That is divine healing.

So it is with every man who is really baptized in the Holy Ghost. Last Wednesday night, as our service was about to commence, I laid my Bible on the table. A man came in and took up the Bible and dropped it as though it was hot.

Then a woman sitting nearby reached out and took it up, and the power of God came upon her and she commenced to shake. They said, "Isn't that strange!" Not at all. That is the Bible over which Brother Westwood and Brother Fogwill and I kneel in the healing rooms and ask God to open its blessed pages, that we may understand the Spirit of the Word of God and receive the power of God that makes these people well. I believe the very paper becomes saturated with the power of God.

Both animate and inanimate objects can become filled with the Spirit of God. Even the bones of those who have trusted in the living God have retained their virtue. The old prophet [Elisha] had been in his grave many a day, when one day in their haste to bury a man, they opened the same grave in which the prophet's bones lay. But when the dead man touched the bones of that Holy Ghost-filled man, he became a living man and rose up well. (See 2 Kings 13:21.)

Oh, the most vital thing in all the universe is the Holy Spirit. It is more real than electricity, more powerful than gravity. It is more subtle than the ether in the air. It contains more energy than any natural power. It is the vitality of the living God, the fire of His soul, the very substance of His being. Bless God! Open your nature to God. Receive the Christ into your heart. Confess your sins and acknowledge the Lord Jesus Christ as your Savior. Receive Him as your Savior and Healer now, and God will bless you.

About the Author

∼∙≺◈≻∙∽

John Graham Lake was born on March 18, 1870, in St. Mary's, Ontario, Canada. While he was still a child, his parents moved to the United States. At the age of twenty-one, he became a Methodist minister; however, he chose to start a newspaper in Harvey, Illinois, instead of accepting a church ministry.

From the newspaper business, Lake expanded his career pursuits by opening a real estate office in Sault Saint Marie, Michigan, and then in 1904 he bought a seat on the Chicago Board of Trade. Through his real estate deals and his business acumen in insurance and investments, Lake amassed a sizeable fortune by today's standards.

In the meantime, his wife Jennie had suffered with a prolonged and progressively debilitating illness, but she was miraculously delivered under the ministry of John Alexander Dowie in April 1898. This experience forever altered the direction of John G. Lake's life and ministry.

During his business life, Lake had made it a practice of speaking somewhere practically every night, after which he joined like-minded friends in seeking the baptism in the Holy Spirit. Finally, while he and another minister were praying for an invalid woman, he experienced profound "currents of power" rushing through his entire being, and the woman was instantaneously healed.

In the spring of 1907, Lake closed his office for good and disposed of his bank accounts and all his real estate holdings by giving everything away to charity. He then began an independent evangelistic work with a single dollar in his pocket, being absolutely dependent on God for his every need. Lake went wherever the Lord directed him, and he and his family and his ministerial team were always well provided for, most often just at the moment when the provision was needed.

Lake is probably best remembered for his missionary work in South Africa, but his ministry in the United States was also powerful. One hundred thousand healings were recorded in five years at the Lake Healing Rooms in Spokane, Washington. Dr. Ruthledge of Washington, D.C., called Spokane "the healthiest city in the world" as a result.

What he accomplished as a result of his intense regard for the Word of God is an example to all Christians of what is possible for any person who will believe and act on the Scriptures.

About the Compiler

⊷◉⊶

Roberts Liardon, author, public speaker, spiritual leader, church historian, and humanitarian, was born in Tulsa, Oklahoma, the first male child born at Oral Roberts University. For this distinction, he was named in honor of the university founder. Thus, from the start of his life, Roberts was destined to be one of the most well-known Christian authors and speakers of the turn of the millennium. To date, he has sold over six million books worldwide in over fifty languages and is internationally renowned.

An author of over four dozen Christian and self-help books, Roberts's career in ministry began when he gave his first public address at the age of thirteen. At seventeen, he published his first book, *I Saw Heaven*, which catapulted him into the public eye. By the time he was eighteen years old, he was one of the leading public speakers in the world. Later, he would write and produce a book and video series entitled *God's Generals*. This became one of the best-selling Christian series in history and established Roberts as a leading Protestant church historian.

In 1990, at the age of twenty-five, Roberts moved to Southern California and established his worldwide headquarters in Orange County. There, he founded Embassy Christian Center, which would become a base for his humanitarian work that would include assistance to the poor and needy, not only in Southern California, but throughout the world. He also built one of the largest Christian churches and Bible colleges in Orange County. He has established, financed, and sent forth more than 250 men and women to various nations. These humanitarian missionary teams have taken food, clothing, and medical supplies, along with the message of Jesus to needy friends and neighbors worldwide.

As a church historian, Roberts also fervently researches our Christian heritage. At age twelve, he received instruction from God to study past heroes of faith and gain insight into their successes and their failures. The pursuit of Christian history became his passion, and, even as a young man, Roberts spent much of his free time with older Christians who knew the likes of William Branham, Kathryn Kuhlman, and Aimee Semple McPherson—great men and women of faith whose stories are told in the first *God's Generals* book and videos. Roberts possesses a wealth of knowledge regarding the great leaders of three Christian movements—Pentecostal, divine healing, and charismatic—and he has established ongoing research through the Reformers and Revivalists Historical Museum in California.

Overall, historian, pastor, teacher, humanitarian, and philanthropist Roberts Liardon has dedicated his entire life and finances to the work of God's kingdom and the welfare of his fellow man, keeping a watchful eye on those less fortunate and doing all he can to ease their pain and help their dreams come to pass.

For speaking engagements you may contact Roberts Liardon at:

Roberts Liardon Ministries
P.O. Box 2989
Sarasota, FL 34230
Phone: 941.373.3883
www.robertsliardon.com

United Kingdom/Europe
22 Notting Hill Gate
Suite 125
London, England W11 3JE
United Kingdom